The Easy Cookbook

The Easy Cookbook

Over 100 Satisfying Recipes

Made with Four Ingredients or Less

CIDER MILL PRESS

BOOK PUBLISHERS

KENNEBUNKPORT, MAINE

Contents

Introduction

For many, their best memories of food are sitting at a table, watching grandma work her magic. Her soft, pleasant singing as the dish came together. The delicious scents of whatever she was making filling the kitchen. The soothing rhythms of her stirring, tasting, calmly adding a pinch of this, a dash of that.

Typically, such recollections make sure to emphasize that she turned out these miraculous dishes with a recipe nowhere in sight.

Despite the lesson offered by these warm memories, many people today are afraid to venture anywhere near the kitchen without an explicit recipe. Since meemaw's too sweet to tell you, we will: cooking is not a formula, but a feeling. It's supposed to be fun, not a crucible constructed to test how well you follow directions.

In reality, your ability to turn out a delicious, wholesome meal (and enjoy yourself as you do) depends on three things: intuition, confidence, and quality ingredients.

We're here to help with the first two. Each of the recipes within is designed to build your skill level by helping you learn to trust your eyes, your palate, and your gut. To do this, we have chosen simple dishes that make it easier for you to pay attention to what's in front of you, and are explicit only about a preparation's essential components—either those ingredients that supply its raison d'etre or have an outsized impact on its flavor.

The rest is placed in your hands so that you can honor grandma's example pinch by pinch, each success bringing you one step closer to ensuring that this grand tradition gets passed along.

This approach allows you to see how a dish comes together. When you work in dashes and pinches rather than stirring in prescribed amounts, it becomes easier to understand what each element brings, and how they can be used to salvage future preparations that are in danger of going awry.

This incremental tinkering also forces you to develop the most valuable habit in quality cooking: tasting as you go, which will develop your palate and your confidence, and allow you to navigate the inevitable shifts in conditions and materials that will have a profound effect on a particular dish. Cooking, as with any craft, is about having the requisite care and attention to remain flexible to the demands of a given situation, and the know-how to resolve the issues that arise.

Over time, using this method, you'll not only become a better cook, but you'll also look to the kitchen as a refuge instead of a gauntlet the demands of the day force you to run. You'll become increasingly creative and confident, buoyed by the age-old balms of ritual, taking personal responsibility for your own well being, and doing something well.

The last piece of cooking's holy trinity—quality ingredients—is on you. Sure, money is almost always a concern. But we're willing to bet that if you spend more time cooking at home, and refrain from going out or getting takeaway, there will always be enough in the coffers to select items that honor the time and energy you're about to expend. There's more than enough to do when preparing a meal. Attempting to carry out the impossible—lifting subpar ingredients to lofty heights—can only result in frustration, and conviction dwindling to dangerously low levels. If you commit to buying the best you can, most of the work is already done for you, meaning that the playful, carefree spirit grandma displayed in the kitchen will be well within reach.

Breakfast

By now, with the hectic pace of the world, most have convinced themselves that there's no time in the morning to prepare something wholesome and delicious. They fall back on ready-made items that go well beside a cup of coffee, but are often counterproductive, sapping, rather than supplying energy.

These preparations solve all of these issues. Quick, wholesome, and delicious, each dish has plenty to offer, including a host of easy-to-grasp techniques that will serve you well in your commitment to improving in the kitchen.

Breakfast Tacos

 +

8 EGGS   6 CORN TORTILLAS,
                      WARMED

Directions

1. Warm a large cast-iron skillet over medium heat. Place the eggs in a mixing bowl, beat until scrambled, and then whisk in the seasonings and cilantro.

2. Coat the bottom of the skillet with butter and add the egg mixture. Scramble until the eggs are fluffy and cooked through.

3. Serve with the tortillas and your favorite taco fixings.

As Needed or To Taste: Chili powder, cumin, adobo seasoning, dried oregano, salt, pepper, chopped fresh cilantro, unsalted butter

Huevos Rancheros

| 4 CORN TORTILLAS | 1 (14 OZ.) CAN OF BLACK BEANS, DRAINED AND RINSED | 8 EGGS | 1 CUP GRATED SHARP CHEDDAR CHEESE |

Directions

1. Coat the bottom of a large cast-iron skillet with olive oil and warm over medium-high heat. When the oil starts to shimmer, add the tortillas and cook until they start to brown. Add the beans and mash them into the tortillas. Cook until the beans are warmed through, about 5 minutes.

2. Break the eggs over the beans, cover the skillet, and cook until the whites start to set, about 2 minutes.

3. Remove the lid, top with the cheese, cover the skillet, and cook until it has melted. Garnish with jalapeños and cilantro and serve with salsa on the side.

As Needed or To Taste: Olive oil, sliced jalapeño peppers, finely chopped fresh cilantro, salsa

Tamagoyaki

 +

4 LARGE EGGS   1 TABLESPOON
                          MIRIN

Directions

1. Place the eggs and mirin in a mixing bowl. Add a pinch of salt and several dashes of soy sauce and whisk to combine.

2. Coat the bottom of a large cast-iron skillet with olive oil and warm it over medium-high heat. When the oil starts to shimmer, pour a thin layer of the egg mixture into the pan, tilting and swirling to make sure the egg completely coats the bottom. When the bottom of the egg is just set and there is still liquid on top, use a chopstick to gently roll the egg up into a log. If you overcook the egg, it won't stick as you roll it.

3. When the first roll is at one end of the pan, pour another thin layer of egg mixture into the pan. When the bottom of this layer is set, move the roll back onto it. Roll the layer up to the other end of the pan. Repeat until all of the egg mixture has been used up. Remove the omelet from the pan and let it set for a few minutes before trimming the ends and slicing it into even pieces.

As Needed or To Taste: Salt, soy sauce, olive oil

Mediterranean Omelet

+

+

4 EGGS

2 TABLESPOONS
RICOTTA

2 TABLESPOONS
CHOPPED OLIVES

Directions

1. Place the eggs in a mixing bowl, beat until scrambled, and season with salt.

2. Warm a skillet over medium heat. Coat the skillet with butter, add the eggs, and shake the pan to evenly distribute them. Cook for 1 or 2 minutes, until the eggs start to set on the bottom.

3. Using a spatula, gently flip the omelet over and immediately place the ricotta in the middle. Top with sun-dried tomatoes and olives and cook for 1 minute. Sprinkle arugula over the omelet, fold it in half, and cook for another 30 seconds.

As Needed or To Taste: Salt, butter, sun-dried tomatoes in olive oil, arugula

Spinach & Feta Frittata

 +  +  +

| 6 EGGS | ½ RED ONION, CHOPPED | 2 CUPS SPINACH, STEMMED AND CHOPPED | ½ CUP CRUMBLED FETA CHEESE |

Directions

1. Set the oven's broiler to low. Place the eggs in a small bowl and beat until scrambled.

2. Warm a small cast-iron skillet over medium-high heat. Coat the bottom with butter and then add the onion and garlic. Sauté until the onion is translucent, about 3 minutes.

3. Add the spinach and cook, stirring continuously, until it wilts, about 2 minutes. Sprinkle the feta over the mixture.

4. Pour the eggs into the skillet and shake the pan to evenly distribute them. Season with salt and pepper, cover the skillet, and cook until set, about 10 minutes.

5. Place the skillet under the broiler and toast the top for about 2 minutes. Remove and let stand for a couple of minutes before serving.

As Needed or To Taste: Unsalted butter, minced garlic, salt, pepper

Green Shakshuka

1 ONION, CHOPPED   ½ LB. TOMATILLOS, HUSKED, RINSED, AND CHOPPED   1 (12 OZ.) PACKAGE OF FROZEN CHOPPED SPINACH   8 EGGS

Directions

1. Coat the bottom of a large skillet with olive oil and warm it over medium-high heat. When the oil starts to shimmer, add the onion and sauté until it just starts to soften, about 5 minutes. Add garlic and cook until fragrant, about 1 minute. Add the tomatillos and cook until they start to collapse, about 5 minutes.

2. Add the spinach and coriander and cook, breaking up the spinach with a fork, until the spinach is completely defrosted and blended with the tomatillos. Season with salt and pepper.

3. Evenly spread the mixture in the pan and then make 8 indentations in it. Crack an egg into each indentation. Reduce the heat to medium, cover the pan, and let the eggs cook until the whites are set, 3 to 5 minutes. Generously sprinkle Tabasco over the top before serving.

As Needed or To Taste: Olive oil, minced garlic, coriander, salt, pepper, Tabasco

Strata

8 EGGS, BEATEN   2 CUPS WHOLE MILK   3 CUPS DAY-OLD BREAD PIECES   1 CUP DICED COOKED HAM

Directions

1. Place the eggs and milk in a large mixing bowl and whisk to combine. Stir in the cheese and nutmeg and then add the bread pieces. Transfer the mixture to the refrigerator and chill for 30 minutes.

2. Preheat the oven to 400°F. Add the ham, onion, and spinach to the egg-and-bread mixture and stir until evenly distributed. Season with salt and pepper.

3. Coat the bottom of a medium cast-iron skillet with olive oil. Pour in the strata, place the skillet in the oven, and bake until it is golden brown and set in the center, about 25 minutes. Remove from the oven and let it rest for 10 minutes before slicing and serving.

    As Needed or To Taste: Shredded Gruyère cheese, freshly grated nutmeg, minced onion, chopped spinach, salt, pepper, olive oil

Chicken Congee

 +  +

4 CUPS CHICKEN STOCK
(SEE PAGE 104)

1½ CUPS
LONG-GRAIN RICE

2 CUPS COOKED AND
SHREDDED CHICKEN BREAST

Directions

1.　Place the stock in a Dutch oven and bring to a simmer over medium heat. Coat a wok or large skillet with olive oil and warm it over medium heat. When the oil starts to shimmer, add garlic and cook until it is fragrant and golden brown, about 2 minutes. Add the rice, stir until coated with the oil, and cook until it is golden brown, about 4 minutes.

2.　Add the rice and garlic to the stock and season with salt and pepper. Cook, stirring occasionally, until the rice is tender, about 20 minutes.

3.　Stir in the chicken and cook until warmed through. Ladle into warmed bowls and garnish with cilantro.

As Needed or To Taste: Olive oil, garlic, salt, pepper, finely chopped fresh cilantro

Ham & Swiss Quiche

 **+** **+** **+**

1 READY-MADE PIE CRUST, BLIND BAKED	8 EGGS	1½ CUPS LIGHT CREAM	½ LB. HONEY-BAKED HAM, DICED

Directions

1. Preheat the oven to 375°F. Place the eggs, cream, salt, pepper, and nutmeg in a mixing and beat until the mixture is combined.

2. Cover the bottom of the pie crust with spinach and Swiss cheese. Top with the ham and pour the egg mixture over the top, shaking the pan gently to make sure it gets evenly distributed.

3. Place the quiche in the oven and bake until the eggs are puffy and starting to brown, about 40 minutes. Remove from the oven and let the quiche rest for 5 minutes before slicing and serving.

As Needed or To Taste: Salt, pepper, freshly grated nutmeg, spinach, shredded Swiss cheese

PB & Banana Yogurt Bowl

 +  +  +

4 CUPS PLAIN GREEK YOGURT + **½ CUP UNSALTED PEANUT BUTTER** + **3 BANANAS** + **4 CUPS BABY SPINACH**

Directions

1. Place the yogurt, peanut butter, bananas, and spinach in a food processor and blitz until smooth.

2. Divide the mixture between the serving bowls and top each portion with chia seeds, coconut, and peanuts.

As Needed or To Taste: Chia seeds, shredded coconut, crushed peanuts

Peanut Butter & Bacon Oats

 +  + +

| 6 SLICES OF THICK-CUT BACON | 2 CUPS STEEL-CUT OATS | 6 EGGS | ¼ CUP CRUNCHY PEANUT BUTTER |

Directions

1. Place the bacon in a large cast-iron skillet and cook over medium heat until crispy, about 8 minutes. Transfer the bacon to a paper towel–lined plate to drain. When the bacon is cool enough to handle, chop it into bite-sized pieces.

2. While the bacon is cooking, place the oats in a large saucepan, cover them with water, and add salt. Cook over medium heat until the oats are tender, about 10 minutes.

3. Place the eggs in the skillet and fry them in the bacon fat until the whites and yolks are set. Stir the bacon and peanut butter into the oats and ladle the mixture into warmed bowls. Top each portion with a fried egg and serve.

As Needed or To Taste: Salt

Chia Seed Pudding

 **+**  **+**  **+**

| 1½ CUPS COCONUT MILK | ½ CUP PLAIN NONFAT GREEK YOGURT | 1 CUP PITTED DARK CHERRIES | ½ CUP CHIA SEEDS |

Directions

1. Place all of the ingredients in a blender and puree until the mixture is the desired consistency. Chill in the refrigerator overnight.

As Needed or To Taste: Chopped dark chocolate, honey, salt

Snacks, Sides & Salads

It doesn't get much easier than cooking a chicken breast, a piece of steak, or a fillet of fish. Having to depend on just that, night after night, is another matter.

The ability to round out your plate with recipes that are either fun, inventive, or fresh and healthy is crucial if you're going to keep things from getting stale when cooking at home. These recipes allow you to do just that, and are a great way to introduce your palate to flavors and textures that will serve you well elsewhere.

Kale Chips

1 BUNCH OF KALE,
STEMS REMOVED

Directions

1. Preheat the oven to 400°F. Tear the kale leaves into smaller pieces and place them in a mixing bowl. Add olive oil, salt, pepper, paprika, dried parsley, dried basil, dried thyme, and dried sage to taste and work the mixture with your hands until the kale pieces are evenly coated.

2. Divide the seasoned kale between 2 parchment-lined baking sheets so that it sits on each in an even layer. Place in the oven and bake until crispy, 6 to 8 minutes. Remove and let cool before serving.

    As Needed or To Taste: Olive oil, salt, pepper, paprika, dried parsley, dried basil, dried thyme, dried sage

Zucchini Rolls

 **+**  **+**  **+**

3 SMALL ZUCCHINI, SLICED INTO ¼-INCH-THICK SLICES   3 TABLESPOONS GOAT CHEESE   2 OZ. BABY SPINACH, FINELY CHOPPED   3 TABLESPOONS PINE NUTS

Directions

1. Preheat the oven to 400°F. Brush the zucchini slices with olive oil and season them with salt and pepper.

2. Place the zucchini on a baking sheet, place it in the oven, and bake until the zucchini starts to brown, about 30 minutes, turning them occasionally. Remove from the oven and let cool.

3. Place the goat cheese in a bowl, add parsley and lemon juice to taste, and stir to combine.

4. Spread the goat cheese mixture over the zucchini. Sprinkle the spinach and pine nuts over the top and add basil to taste. Roll the slices up, secure the rolls with toothpicks, and serve.

As Needed or To Taste: Olive oil, salt, pepper, finely chopped fresh parsley, fresh lemon juice, finely chopped fresh basil

Traditional Hummus

 + +

1 (14 OZ.) CAN OF
CHICKPEAS

3 TABLESPOONS
OLIVE OIL

3 TABLESPOONS
TAHINI

Directions

1. Drain the chickpeas and reserve the liquid. If time allows, remove the skins from each of the chickpeas. This will make your hummus much smoother.

2. Place the chickpeas, olive oil, and tahini in a food processor, add lemon juice, garlic, salt, and pepper to taste, and blitz until the mixture is very smooth, scraping down the work bowl as needed.

3. Taste and adjust the seasoning as necessary. If your hummus is thicker than you'd like, add 2 to 3 tablespoons of the reserved chickpea liquid and blitz until it is the desired consistency.

As Needed or To Taste: Fresh lemon juice, chopped garlic, salt, pepper

Hummus Variations

For a more authentic hummus, soak dried chickpeas overnight and then cook them until very tender, about 1 hour. You can also dress your hummus up with any of the following options: add 1 to 3 teaspoons of spices like cumin, sumac, harissa, or smoked paprika; blend in 1 cup of roasted eggplant, zucchini, bell peppers, or garlic; or fold in ¾ cup of chopped green or black olives.

Roasted Tomato Salsa

**1 LB. TOMATOES,
HALVED AND CORED**

Directions

1. Preheat the oven to 450°F. Place the tomatoes in a large bowl, add olive oil, salt, and pepper to taste, and toss to coat. Let the mixture stand at room temperature for 30 minutes.

2. Place the tomatoes, cut side down, on a baking sheet, place them in the oven, and roast until they start to char and soften, about 10 minutes. Carefully turn the tomatoes over and cook until they start bubbling, about 5 minutes. Remove from the oven and let the tomatoes cool completely.

3. Chop the tomatoes and place them in a bowl. Add onion, jalapeño, cilantro, and lime juice to taste, stir to combine, and let the salsa stand at room temperature for 45 minutes.

4. Taste, adjust seasoning as necessary, and serve.

As Needed or To Taste: Olive oil, salt, pepper, minced onion, minced jalapeño pepper, finely chopped fresh cilantro, fresh lime juice

Mushroom Toast with Whipped Goat Cheese

 +  + +

| ½ LB. MUSHROOMS (CHESTNUT RECOMMENDED), SLICED | 4 THICK SLICES OF SOUROUGH BREAD | ½ CUP HEAVY CREAM | 4 OZ. GOAT CHEESE, AT ROOM TEMPERATURE |

Directions

1. Preheat the oven to 400°F. Place the mushrooms on a baking sheet, drizzle olive oil over them, and season with salt. Place the mushrooms in the oven and roast until they begin to darken, about 10 to 15 minutes. Place the slices of bread on another baking sheet, brush the tops with oil, and season with salt. Place the slices of bread in the oven and bake until golden brown, about 10 minutes.

2. While the mushrooms and bread are in the oven, place the cream in a mixing bowl and beat until stiff peaks begin to form. Add the goat cheese and beat until well combined.

3. Remove the mushrooms and bread from the oven and let cool for 5 minutes. Spread the cream-and-goat cheese mixture on the bread and top with the mushrooms. Sprinkle sunflower seeds and rosemary over each piece and top with honey.

As Needed or To Taste: Olive oil, salt, sunflower seeds, finely chopped fresh rosemary, honey

Zucchini Fritters

1½ LBS. ZUCCHINI + **¼ CUP ALL-PURPOSE FLOUR** + **¼ CUP GRATED PARMESAN CHEESE** + **1 EGG, BEATEN**

Directions

1. Line a colander with cheesecloth and grate the zucchini into the colander. Generously sprinkle salt over the zucchini, stir to combine, and let the zucchini drain for 1 hour. After 1 hour, press down on the zucchini to remove as much liquid from it as you can.

2. Place the zucchini, flour, Parmesan, and egg in a mixing bowl and stir to combine. Use your hands to form handfuls of the mixture into balls and then gently press down on the balls to form them into patties.

3. Coat the bottom of a cast-iron skillet with olive oil and warm it over medium-high heat. Working in batches, place the patties in the oil, taking care not to crowd the skillet. Cook until golden brown, about 5 minutes. Flip the patties over and cook for another 5 minutes, until the fritters are also golden brown on that side. Remove from the skillet, transfer to a paper towel–lined plate, and repeat with the remaining patties. If the skillet starts to look dry, add more olive oil. When all of the fritters have been cooked, season with salt and pepper and serve.

As Needed or To Taste: Salt, olive oil, pepper

Spanish Potato Tortilla

 +  +

5 LARGE RUSSET POTATOES, PEELED AND SLICED THIN   1 SPANISH ONION, PEELED AND SLICED   10 EGGS, AT ROOM TEMPERATURE

Directions

1. Place the potatoes and onion in a large cast-iron skillet. Cover the vegetables with olive oil and warm over medium-low heat until the oil comes to a gentle simmer. Cook until the potatoes are tender, about 30 minutes. Remove from heat and let cool slightly.

2. Use a slotted spoon to remove the potatoes and onion from the oil. Reserve the oil. Place the eggs in a large bowl and beat until scrambled. Season with salt and stir in the potatoes and onion.

3. Warm the skillet over high heat. Add ¼ cup of the reserved oil and swirl to coat the bottom and sides of the pan. Pour the egg-and-potato mixture into the pan and stir vigorously to ensure that the mixture does not stick to the sides. Cook for 1 minute and remove the pan from heat. Place the pan over low heat, cover it, and cook for 3 minutes.

4. Carefully invert the tortilla onto a large plate. Return it to the skillet, cook for 3 minutes, and then invert it onto the plate. Return it to the skillet and cook for another 3 minutes. Remove the tortilla from the pan and let it rest at room temperature for 1 hour. Slice into wedges and serve.

As Needed or To Taste: Olive oil, salt

Tiropitakia

½ LB. FETA CHEESE

+

**1 CUP GRATED
KEFALOTYRI CHEESE**

+

2 EGGS, BEATEN

+

**1 (1 LB.) PACKAGE OF FROZEN
PHYLLO DOUGH, THAWED**

Directions

1. Place the feta cheese in a mixing bowl and break it up with a fork. Add the kefalotyri, parsley, eggs, and pepper and stir to combine. Set the mixture aside.

2. Place 1 sheet of the phyllo dough on a large sheet of parchment paper. Gently brush the sheet with some melted butter, place another sheet on top, and brush this with more butter. Cut the phyllo dough into 2-inch strips, place 1 teaspoon of the filling at the end of the strip closest to you, and fold over one corner to make a triangle. Fold the strip up until the filling is completely covered. Repeat with the remaining sheets of phyllo dough and filling.

3. Preheat the oven to 350°F and coat a baking sheet with butter. Place the pastries on the baking sheet and bake in the oven until golden brown, about 15 minutes. Remove and let cool briefly before serving.

As Needed or To Taste: Finely chopped fresh parsley, pepper, melted unsalted butter

Roman-Style Artichokes

**2 LARGE
ARTICHOKES**

Directions

1. Prepare the artichokes by using a serrated knife to cut off the top half with the leaves and all but the last inch of the stem; continue whittling away the outer leaves until you see the hairy-looking choke within. Using a paring knife, peel the outer layer away from the remaining part of the stem; cut the remaining artichoke into quarters and remove the hairy part in the middle. You should have the heart with a little bit of lower leaves left. Place in a bowl of water, add a dash of lemon juice, and set the artichokes aside.

2. Bring water to a boil in a small saucepan. Add the artichokes and parboil until they begin to get tender, 3 to 5 minutes. Remove from the water and drain.

3. Place another small pot on the stove and add enough vegetable oil that the artichoke hearts will be submerged. Warm the oil over medium heat until it starts to sizzle. Add the artichokes to the oil and fry until they are brown all over, turning occasionally, 8 to 10 minutes. Transfer to a paper towel–lined plate to drain. Season with salt and serve with lemon wedges and, if desired, the Lemon-Pepper Mayonnaise.

    As Needed or To Taste: Fresh lemon juice, vegetable oil, salt, lemon wedges, Lemon-Pepper Mayonnaise (optional, see sidebar)

Lemon-Pepper Mayonnaise

Place 1 cup mayonnaise, 3 tablespoons grated Parmesan cheese, 1 tablespoon lemon zest, 3 tablespoons fresh lemon juice, 1½ teaspoons black pepper, and 2 teaspoons kosher salt in a mixing bowl and whisk until combined.

Falafel

 +  +  +

| 1½ (14 OZ.) CANS OF CHICKPEAS, DRAINED AND RINSED | 3 GARLIC CLOVES | ¼ CUP ALL-PURPOSE FLOUR | 1 TEASPOON BAKING SODA |

Directions

1. Place the chickpeas, garlic, flour, and baking soda in a food processor along with onion, parsley, lemon juice, coriander, cumin, salt, and cayenne to taste. Blitz until the mixture is a smooth paste, scraping the work bowl as necessary. Form the mixture into 1-inch balls, place them on a parchment-lined baking sheet, cover tightly with plastic wrap, and refrigerate for 20 minutes.

2. Add vegetable oil to a Dutch oven until it is approximately 2 inches deep and warm to 375°F over medium-high heat. Working in batches, add the falafel and fry until browned all over, about 3 minutes. Transfer the cooked falafel to a paper towel–lined plate to drain. When all of the falafel have been cooked, serve with pita bread and hummus.

As Needed or To Taste: Chopped onion, finely chopped fresh parsley, fresh lemon juice, coriander, cumin, salt, cayenne pepper, vegetable oil, pita bread, hummus

Stuffed Tomatoes

6 LARGE TOMATOES + 1 RED ONION, CHOPPED + ½ GREEN BELL PEPPER, STEMMED, SEEDS AND RIBS REMOVED, AND CHOPPED + ½ CUP COOKED LONG-GRAIN RICE

Directions

1. Cut off the tops of the tomatoes and use a spoon to scoop out the insides, making sure to leave an approximately ¼-inch-thick wall in each of them. Sprinkle salt into the cavities and turn the tomatoes upside down on a paper towel–lined plate. Let stand for about 30 minutes.

2. Coat a large cast-iron skillet with olive oil and warm it over medium-high heat. When the oil starts to shimmer, add the onion, garlic, and bell pepper and sauté until the onion is translucent, about 3 minutes. Season the mixture with cumin, oregano, allspice, nutmeg, salt, and pepper and remove the pan from heat.

3. Set the oven's broiler to high. Transfer the onion mixture to a mixing bowl, stir in the rice, and, add red pepper flakes, parsley, and mint to taste. Fill the tomatoes' cavities with the

mixture, wipe out the skillet, and arrange the stuffed tomatoes in the pan.

4. Place the stuffed tomatoes under the broiler and cook until the tops start to blister, about 5 minutes. Remove from the oven and serve immediately.

As Needed or To Taste: Salt, pepper, olive oil, minced garlic, cumin, finely chopped fresh oregano, allspice, freshly grated nutmeg, red pepper flakes, finely chopped fresh parsley, finely chopped fresh mint

Honey-Glazed Carrots

 **+**

4 CARROTS, PEELED   2 TABLESPOONS HONEY
AND CHOPPED

Directions

1. Preheat the oven to 400°F. Place the carrots and honey in a bowl, add olive oil, cumin, ginger, and cinnamon to taste, and stir until the carrots are evenly coated.

2. Place the carrots on a parchment-lined baking sheet and season with salt and pepper. Place the carrots in the oven and roast until they are tender and lightly browned, about 20 minutes. Remove from the oven and let cool briefly before serving.

    As Needed or To Taste: Olive oil, cumin, ground ginger, cinnamon, salt, pepper

Brussels Sprouts & Hazelnuts

¼ CUP HAZELNUTS   ½ LB. BRUSSELS SPROUTS, TRIMMED AND HALVED

Directions

1. Place the hazelnuts in a large, dry skillet and toast over medium heat until they just start to brown, about 5 minutes. Transfer the nuts to a clean, dry kitchen towel, fold the towel over the nuts, and rub them together until the skins have loosened. Remove the cleaned nuts, discard the skins, and chop the toasted hazelnuts.

2. Place the Brussels sprouts in the skillet, cut side down, and cook over medium heat until slightly charred, about 6 minutes. Turn the Brussels sprouts over, cook for 2 minutes, and place them in a mixing bowl. Drizzle olive oil, lemon juice, and maple syrup over the top. Season with salt, add the hazelnuts, toss to combine, and serve.

As Needed or To Taste: Olive oil, fresh lemon juice, real maple syrup, salt

Charred Eggplant with Feta

 +

2 LARGE EGGPLANTS   ¼ CUP CRUMBLED FETA CHEESE

Directions

1. Set the oven's broiler to high. Place the eggplants on a baking sheet and place it under the broiler. Broil, while turning occasionally, until the eggplants have collapsed and are charred all over, about 10 minutes. Remove from the oven, transfer the eggplants to a large bowl, and cover the bowl with plastic wrap. Let the eggplants steam for 10 minutes.

2. When the eggplants are cool enough to handle, peel off the skin, cut off the ends, and discard. Roughly chop the remaining flesh and return it to the large bowl. Add salt, pepper, olive oil, balsamic glaze, red pepper flakes, and oregano to taste, stir to combine, and sprinkle the feta over the top.

   As Needed or To Taste: Salt, pepper, olive oil, balsamic glaze, red pepper flakes, finely chopped fresh oregano

Lemon Cauliflower Rice

1 HEAD OF CAULIFLOWER, CHOPPED

+

3 TABLESPOONS FRESH LEMON JUICE

+

1 TABLESPOON LEMON ZEST

Directions

1. Place the pieces of cauliflower in a food processor and blitz until granular.

2. Coat a large skillet with olive oil and warm it over medium-high heat. When the oil starts to shimmer, add the cauliflower and cook, stirring occasionally until it starts to brown, about 8 minutes.

3. Season with salt, stir in the lemon juice and lemon zest, and cook, stirring occasionally, until the "rice" is fragrant and warmed through, about 4 minutes.

As Needed or To Taste: Olive oil, salt

Roasted Roots with Ras el Hanout & Honey

| 4 LARGE PARSNIPS, PEELED, TRIMMED, CORED, AND CHOPPED | 4 LARGE CARROTS, PEELED AND SLICED LENGTHWISE | 2 TABLESPOONS HONEY | 1 TABLESPOON RAS EL HANOUT |

Directions

1. Preheat the oven to 400°F. Place the carrots and parsnips in a roasting pan in a single layer, drizzle olive oil over them, and season with salt and pepper. Stir to combine, place the pan in the oven, and roast for about 25 minutes, or until the vegetables are starting to brown.

2. Remove the pan from the oven and gather the vegetables into a pile in the center of the pan. Drizzle the honey over the pile and stir until the vegetables are evenly coated. Sprinkle the Ras el Hanout over the vegetables and stir until evenly distributed.

3. Return the pan to the oven and roast the vegetables for another 5 to 10 minutes, until the vegetables are well browned and cooked through. Remove from the oven and let the vegetables cool briefly before serving.

As Needed or To Taste: Olive oil, salt, pepper

Roasted Beans with Mint & Feta

 +  +  +

½ LB. FRESH GREEN BEANS, TRIMMED   ½ LB. FRESH WAX BEANS, TRIMMED   1 CUP CHERRY TOMATOES, HALVED   ½ CUP CRUMBLED FETA CHEESE

Directions

1. Preheat the oven to 400°F. Place the beans in a large mixing bowl, add olive oil, allspice, cayenne, salt, and pepper to taste, and stir until the beans are evenly coated.

2. Place the beans in a baking dish, place it in the oven, and roast until the beans are al dente, 20 to 25 minutes. Remove from the oven and return them to the large mixing bowl.

3. Stir in the tomatoes and feta, add mint and vinegar to taste, and toss to combine.

As Needed or To Taste: Olive oil, allspice, cayenne pepper, salt, pepper, finely chopped fresh mint, red wine vinegar

Basil Pesto

¼ CUP PINE NUT3   2 CUPS PACKED   ½ CUP OLIVE OIL   ½ CUP GRATED
                         FRESH BASIL LEAVES   PARMESAN CHEESE

Directions

1. Warm a small skillet over low heat for 1 minute. Add the pine nuts and cook, while stirring, until they begin to give off a toasted fragrance, 2 to 3 minutes. Transfer to a plate and let cool completely.

2. Place the pine nuts in a food processor or blender, add garlic and salt, and pulse until the mixture is a coarse meal. Add the basil and pulse until finely minced. Transfer the mixture to a medium bowl and add the oil in a thin stream while whisking to incorporate.

3. Stir in the Parmesan, taste, and adjust the seasoning as necessary.

As Needed or To Taste: Garlic, salt

Garlic & Chili Broccolini

 **+**

½ LB. BROCCOLINI,
TRIMMED

2 GARLIC CLOVES,
MINCED

Directions

1. Bring water to a boil in a large cast-iron skillet. Add the broccolini and cook for 30 seconds. Drain and transfer the broccolini to a paper towel–lined plate.

2. Coat the skillet with olive oil and warm it over medium-high heat. When the oil starts to shimmer, add the broccolini and cook until well browned. Turn the broccolini over, add the garlic, season with salt and pepper, and toss to combine. When the broccolini is browned all over, season with red pepper flakes and toss to evenly distribute. Transfer to a serving platter and garnish with toasted almonds before serving.

As Needed or To Taste: Olive oil, salt, pepper, red pepper flakes, toasted almonds

Raw Beet Salad

 +  +  +

6 RED BEETS, PEELED, TRIMMED, AND GRATED

ZEST AND SEGMENTS OF 1 BLOOD ORANGE

1 LB. ARUGULA

½ LB. BRIE CHEESE, CHOPPED

Directions

1. Place the shredded beets and jalapeño in a salad bowl, season with salt, and stir to combine. Stir in the blood orange zest and segments and then add olive oil, honey, and rice vinegar until the salad is to taste. Cover the salad bowl with plastic wrap and refrigerate overnight.

2. To serve, stir the arugula into the salad and top it with the Brie.

As Needed or To Taste: Minced jalapeño pepper, salt, olive oil, honey, rice vinegar

Mediterranean Tuna Salad

 +  +  +

3 (5 OZ.) CANS OF TUNA IN OLIVE OIL, DRAINED

3 CELERY STALKS, PEELED AND DICED

1 RED BELL PEPPER, STEMMED, SEEDS AND RIBS REMOVED, AND DICED

1 CUP FRESH PARSLEY, CHOPPED

Directions

1. Place the tuna, celery, bell pepper, and parsley in a mixing bowl and stir to combine. Incorporate cucumber, scallions, mint, salt, pepper, mustard, vinegar, olive oil, sumac powder, and red pepper flakes one at a time. Serve with pita bread or mesclun greens.

   As Needed or To Taste: Diced cucumber, diced scallions, diced red onion, finely chopped fresh mint, salt, pepper, Dijon mustard, white vinegar, olive oil, sumac powder, red pepper flakes, pita bread, mesclun greens

Spicy Bean Sprout Salad

¾ LB. BEAN SPROUTS

+

2 SCALLIONS, TRIMMED AND SLICED THIN

+

ZEST OF 1 ORANGE

Directions

1. Bring water to a boil in a small saucepan. Add the bean sprouts and cook for 2 minutes. Drain and let cool.

2. Place the bean sprouts, scallions, and orange zest in a salad bowl, add sesame seeds, sesame oil, soy sauce, red pepper flakes, and ground ginger to taste, and gently stir to combine.

   As Needed or To Taste: Sesame seeds, sesame oil, soy sauce, red pepper flakes, ground ginger

Peppers Stuffed with Feta, Olive & Basil Salad

 +  +  +

| 4 YELLOW BELL PEPPERS, HALVED AND SEEDED | 12 CHERRY TOMATOES, HALVED | ½ CUP CRUMBLED FETA CHEESE | 1 CUP BLACK OLIVES, PITTED |

Directions

1. Preheat the oven to 375°F and place the peppers on a parchment-lined baking sheet. Place the cherry tomatoes, feta, and black olives in a mixing bowl and stir to combine. Add garlic and olive oil to taste, toss to combine, and divide the mixture between the peppers. Place them in the oven and roast until the peppers start to collapse, 10 to 15 minutes.

2. Remove the peppers from the oven and let them cool slightly. Season with salt and pepper and sprinkle basil leaves over the top before serving.

As Needed or To Taste: Minced garlic, olive oil, salt, pepper, fresh basil leaves

Horiatiki Salad

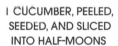
+

+

+

| I CUCUMBER, PEELED, SEEDED, AND SLICED INTO HALF-MOONS | 1 CUP CHERRY TOMATOES, HALVED | 1 CUP CRUMBLED FETA CHEESE | ½ CUP KALAMATA OLIVES, PITTED AND SLICED |

Directions

1. Place the cucumber, cherry tomatoes, feta, and olives in a mixing bowl and stir to combine. Add red onion and oregano to taste and stir to incorporate.

2. Drizzle olive oil over the salad, season with salt and pepper, and gently toss to combine.

As Needed or To Taste: Chopped red onion, dried oregano, olive oil, salt, pepper

Chilled Corn Salad

 +  +

4 CUPS CORN KERNELS   ½ CUP GOAT CHEESE   2 TABLESPOONS
SOUR CREAM

Directions

1. Place the corn, goat cheese, and sour cream in a large mixing bowl and stir to combine. Add unsalted butter, jalapeño pepper, mayonnaise, garlic powder, cayenne pepper, chili powder, lime juice, cilantro, salt, and pepper to taste and stir to combine.

2. Place the salad in the refrigerator and refrigerate for 3 hours. Serve over lettuce or arugula.

    As Needed or To Taste: Unsalted butter, minced jalapeño pepper, mayonnaise, garlic powder, cayenne pepper, chili powder, fresh lime juice, finely chopped fresh cilantro, salt, pepper, lettuce or arugula

Curried Chicken Salad

 +  +  +

| 4 CUPS DICED, COOKED CHICKEN | 3 CELERY STALKS, PEELED AND MINCED | 2 GRANNY SMITH APPLES, MINCED | ½ RED BELL PEPPER, STEMMED, SEEDS AND RIBS REMOVED, AND MINCED |

Directions

1. Place the chicken in a mixing bowl, add the desired amount of mayonnaise, and stir to combine. Season to taste with lime juice, curry powder, cumin, garlic powder, cinnamon, turmeric, salt, and pepper and then stir in the celery, apples, and bell pepper.

2. Top with chopped pecans and serve over arugula or with slices of toasted bread.

As Needed or To Taste: Mayonnaise, fresh lime juice, curry powder, cumin, garlic powder, cinnamon, turmeric, salt, pepper, chopped pecans, arugula, slices of toasted bread

Chickpea Salad

2 CUPS DRIED CHICKPEAS, SOAKED OVERNIGHT

+

1 ONION, CHOPPED

+

1 CUP FINELY CHOPPED FRESH CILANTRO

+

½ CUP SUN-DRIED TOMATOES IN OLIVE OIL, DRAINED

Directions

1. Drain the chickpeas, place them in a saucepan, and cover them with stock. Bring to a boil, reduce the heat, and simmer until the chickpeas are tender, about 45 minutes. Drain the chickpeas and let them cool completely.

2. Place the chickpeas, onion, cilantro, and sun-dried tomatoes in a salad bowl, stir to combine, and add olive oil, lemon juice, saffron, cumin, cinnamon, red pepper flakes, salt, and pepper to taste. Toss until combined and serve.

As Needed or To Taste: Chicken Stock (see page 104), olive oil, fresh lemon juice, saffron, cumin, cinnamon, red pepper flakes, salt, pepper

Watermelon & Feta Salad

 **+**  **+**

FLESH OF ½ WATERMELON, CUBED   1 CUCUMBER, DICED   ½ CUP CRUMBLED FETA CHEESE

Directions

1. Place the watermelon and cucumber in a salad bowl, add mint, basil, honey, lemon juice, olive oil, and salt to taste, and toss to combine.

2. Top with the feta and serve.

    As Needed or To Taste: Fresh mint leaves, fresh basil leaves, honey, fresh lemon juice, olive oil, salt

Soups

The feelings of comfort closely associated with soup are a surprise to no one. What may surprise the developing cook is how much valuable insight the preparation of a flavorful, nourishing broth offers.

The value of careful seasoning, having the patience to let flavors develop, and planning ahead—making sure you always have homemade stock on hand, for instance—will quickly become clear as you work your way through the recipes in this chapter, meaning that you will not only feel consoled after making them, but more confident as well.

Creamed Asparagus Soup with Bacon

½ LB. BACON + 1 ONION, CHOPPED + 2 BUNCHES OF ASPARAGUS, TRIMMED AND CHOPPED + 4 GARLIC CLOVES, SLICED THIN

Directions

1. Place the bacon in a medium saucepan and cook over medium heat until crispy, about 8 minutes. Transfer the bacon to a paper towel-lined plate and drain almost all of the rendered fat from the pan. When the bacon is cool enough to handle, chop it into bite-sized pieces.

2. Melt butter in the saucepan over medium heat. Add the onion and sauté until it is translucent, about 3 minutes. Set the asparagus tips aside. Add the garlic and the remaining asparagus to the onion, fill the pan halfway with stock, and bring to a simmer. Cook until the asparagus is tender, about 20 minutes.

3. While the soup is simmering, bring water to a boil in a saucepan. Add salt and the asparagus tips and cook them for 2 minutes. Drain, run the asparagus tips under cold water, and set them aside.

4. Transfer the soup to a blender and puree until smooth. Season it with salt, pour it into warmed bowls, and top with the bacon and asparagus tips. Garnish each portion with a drizzle of buttermilk.

As Needed or To Taste: Unsalted butter, Chicken Stock (see page 104), salt, buttermilk

Butternut Squash & Chorizo Bisque

| 1 LARGE BUTTERNUT SQUASH, PEELED, SEEDED, AND SLICED | 1 ONION, SLICED | ½ LB. CHORIZO, CASING REMOVED | 2 CUPS WHOLE MILK |

Directions

1. Preheat the oven to 400°F. Place the squash and onion in a bowl, drizzle olive oil over the mixture, and season with salt. Toss to combine, place the mixture in a baking dish, and roast until the onion is browned, about 15 minutes. Remove the dish from the oven, transfer the onion to a bowl, return the squash to the oven, and roast until the squash is fork-tender, another 30 minutes or so. Remove from the oven and transfer to the bowl containing the onion.

2. Coat a large skillet with olive oil and warm it over medium-high heat. When the oil starts to shimmer, add the chorizo and cook, turning occasionally, until it is browned all over, about 5 minutes. Remove and set on a paper towel–lined plate to drain. When cool enough to handle, chop the chorizo into bite-sized pieces.

3. Place the squash, onion, chorizo, and milk in a large saucepan, add salt, pepper, stock, and bay leaves as desired, and bring to a boil over medium-high heat, stirring often. Reduce heat so that the soup simmers and cook for another 20 minutes.

4. Remove the bay leaves, transfer the soup to a blender, and puree until smooth. Return the soup to the saucepan and bring to a simmer. Add butter until the soup has the desired texture, stir until it has melted, and then ladle the soup into warmed bowls.

As Needed or To Taste: Olive oil, salt, pepper, Vegetable Stock (see page 103), bay leaves, unsalted butter

Lamb & Lentil Soup

| 1 LB. LEG OF LAMB, CUT INTO 1-INCH PIECES | 1 ONION, MINCED | 1 POTATO, PEELED AND CHOPPED | ½ CUP RED LENTILS |

Directions

1. Fill a large saucepan halfway with stock and bring it to a boil. Reduce the heat so that the stock simmers and stir in the lamb and onion. Add garlic, bay leaves, cloves, and thyme to taste and simmer the soup until the lamb is tender, about 45 minutes.

2. Remove the bay leaves, sprigs of thyme, and cloves, add the potato and lentils, cover the pan, and cook until the lentils and potato are tender, about 15 minutes. Season the soup with salt and pepper, add parsley to taste, and ladle the soup into warmed bowls.

As Needed or To Taste: Vegetable Stock (see sidebar), minced garlic, bay leaves, whole cloves, sprigs of fresh thyme, salt, pepper, finely chopped fresh parsley

Vegetable Stock

Place 2 tablespoons olive oil, 2 trimmed and well-rinsed leeks, 2 peeled and sliced carrots, 2 celery stalks, 2 sliced onions, and 3 unpeeled, smashed garlic cloves in a large stockpot and cook over low heat until the liquid the vegetables release has evaporated. Add 2 sprigs of fresh parsley and thyme, 1 bay leaf, 8 cups water, ½ teaspoon black peppercorns, and salt to taste. Raise the heat to high and bring the stock to a boil. Reduce heat so that the stock simmers and cook for 2 hours, skimming to remove any impurities that float to the surface. Strain the stock through a fine sieve, let the stock cool slightly, and place it in the refrigerator, uncovered, to chill. Remove the fat layer and cover. The stock will keep in the refrigerator for 3 to 5 days, and in the freezer for up to 3 months.

Chicken Stock

Place 3 lbs. rinsed chicken bones in a large stockpot, cover them with water, and bring to a boil. Add 1 chopped onion, 2 chopped carrots, 3 chopped celery stalks, 3 unpeeled, smashed garlic cloves, 3 sprigs of fresh thyme, 1 teaspoon black peppercorns, 1 bay leaf, and salt to taste, and reduce the heat so that the stock simmers. Cook for 2 hours, skimming to remove any impurities that float to the surface. Strain the stock through a fine sieve, let the stock cool slightly, and place it in the refrigerator, uncovered, to chill. Remove the fat layer and cover. The stock will keep in the refrigerator for 3 to 5 days, and in the freezer for up to 3 months.

Split Pea Soup with Smoked Ham

 **+**  **+** **+**

| 1 ONION, MINCED | 1 CARROT, PEELED AND MINCED | 1 CUP SPLIT PEAS | ½ LB. SMOKED HAM, CHOPPED |

Directions

1. Warm a large saucepan over medium heat. Coat the saucepan with butter, add the onion and carrot, and sauté until they have softened, about 5 minutes.

2. Fill the pan halfway with stock and stir in the split peas and ham. Add parsley, bay leaves, and thyme to taste, bring the soup to a boil, and reduce the heat to medium-low. Simmer the soup, stirring occasionally, until the peas are al dente, about 1 hour.

3. Remove the bay leaves and discard. Season the soup with salt and pepper and ladle it into warmed bowls. Garnish with additional parsley and serve with lemon wedges.

As Needed or To Taste: Unsalted butter, Chicken Stock (see sidebar), finely chopped fresh parsley, bay leaves, finely chopped fresh thyme, salt, pepper, lemon wedges

Mansaf

1 ONION, CHOPPED   2 LBS. LAMB SHOULDER, CUBED   1 CUP PLAIN GREEK YOGURT   2 CUPS COOKED LONG-GRAIN RICE

Directions

1. Coat the bottom of a large saucepan with olive oil and warm it over medium-high heat. When the oil starts to shimmer, add the onion and sauté until it starts to soften, about 5 minutes. Add the lamb and cook, turning it occasionally, until it is browned all over, about 8 minutes.

2. Fill the pan halfway with stock and bring the soup to a boil. Add cardamom seeds to taste, reduce the heat to medium-low, cover the pan, and simmer until the lamb is very tender, about 1 hour.

3. Stir in the yogurt, season the soup with salt and pepper, and remove the pan from heat. Divide the rice between the serving bowls, ladle the soup over the rice, and garnish with toasted pine nuts and parsley.

    As Needed or To Taste: Olive oil, Beef Stock (see sidebar), cardamom seeds, salt, pepper, toasted pine nuts, finely chopped fresh parsley

Beef Stock

Place 3 lbs. beef bones in a stockpot and cover with cold water. Bring to a simmer over medium-high heat, skimming to remove any impurities that float to the surface. Reduce the heat to low, add 2 chopped yellow onions, 3 chopped carrots, 4 chopped celery stalks, 3 crushed garlic cloves, 3 sprigs of fresh thyme, 1 teaspoon whole black peppercorns, 1 bay leaf, and salt to taste, and simmer for 5 hours, skimming to remove any impurities that float to the surface. Strain, let cool slightly, and transfer to the refrigerator. Leave uncovered and let cool completely. Remove the layer of fat and cover. The stock will keep in the refrigerator for 3 to 5 days, and in the freezer for up to 3 months.

Eggplant & Zucchini Soup

I LARGE EGGPLANT, PEELED AND CHOPPED + 2 LARGE ZUCCHINI, CHOPPED + 3 GARLIC CLOVES, MINCED + 1 ONION, CHOPPED

Directions

1. Preheat the oven to 425°F. Place the eggplant, zucchini, onion, and garlic in a baking dish, drizzle the olive oil over the mixture, and gently stir to coat. Place the vegetables in the oven and roast until they are tender, about 30 minutes, stirring occasionally. Remove from the oven and let the vegetables cool briefly.

2. Place half of the roasted vegetables in a food processor and puree until smooth, adding stock as needed. Place the puree in a medium saucepan, fill the pan halfway with stock, and stir in the remaining roasted vegetables. Bring the soup to a boil.

3. Add oregano, mint, salt, and pepper to taste and simmer the soup for 2 minutes. Ladle into warmed bowls, garnish with additional mint, and serve with bread.

As Needed or To Taste: Olive oil, Vegetable Stock (see page 103), finely chopped fresh oregano, finely chopped fresh mint, salt, pepper, bread

Smoked Chorizo & Cabbage Soup

1 ONION, CHOPPED

1 LB. DRIED SMOKED CHORIZO, SLICED

1 HEAD OF GREEN CABBAGE, CORED AND SLICED

1 TABLESPOON CUMIN SEEDS

Directions

1. Coat the bottom of a large saucepan with olive oil and warm it over medium heat. When the oil starts to shimmer, add the onion and sauté until it starts to soften, about 5 minutes.

2. Add the chorizo, cabbage, and cumin seeds and cook until the cabbage starts to wilt, about 5 minutes, stirring frequently. Fill the pan halfway with stock, raise the heat to high, and bring the soup to a boil. Reduce the heat so that the soup simmers and cook for an additional 10 minutes.

3. Season the soup with cinnamon, salt, and pepper and ladle it into warmed bowls.

As Needed or To Taste: Olive oil, fresh thyme leaves, Chicken Stock (see page 104), cinnamon, salt, pepper

Baby Spinach & Yogurt Soup

1 ONION, CHOPPED   10 OZ. BABY SPINACH   ¼ CUP LONG-GRAIN RICE   1½ CUPS WHOLE-MILK YOGURT

Directions

1. Coat the bottom of a large saucepan with olive oil and warm it over medium heat. When the oil starts to shimmer, add the onion and sauté until it starts to soften, about 5 minutes.

2. Add two-thirds of the spinach, cover the pan, and cook until all the spinach is wilted, about 2 minutes.

3. Add the rice, fill the pan halfway with stock, and add scallions to taste. Simmer until the rice is tender, about 18 minutes.

4. Transfer the soup to a food processor or blender, add garlic and turmeric to taste along with the remaining spinach, and puree until smooth. Return the soup to a clean saucepan, bring it to a simmer, and stir in the yogurt. Season the soup with salt and pepper, ladle it into warm bowls, and drizzle additional olive oil over each portion.

As Needed or To Taste: Olive oil, chopped scallions, Vegetable Stock (see page 103), minced garlic, turmeric, salt, pepper

Butternut Squash, Quinoa & Chicken Soup

 +  + +

1 BUTTERNUT SQUASH, HALVED AND SEEDED

2 CHICKEN BREASTS, CUT INTO ½-INCH CUBES

1 (14 OZ.) CAN OF STEWED TOMATOES, DRAINED AND CHOPPED

⅔ CUP QUINOA, RINSED

Directions

1. Preheat the oven to 375°F. Place the butternut squash, cut side up, on a baking sheet, drizzle olive oil over it, and place it in the oven. Roast until the flesh is very tender, about 45 minutes. Remove from the oven and let cool.

2. Coat the bottom of a Dutch oven with olive oil and warm it over medium heat. When the oil starts to shimmer, add the chicken and cook, turning frequently, until it is browned all over, about 6 minutes. Remove the chicken with a slotted spoon and set it aside.

3. Cover the bottom of the pot with onion and sauté until it has softened, about 5 minutes. Add garlic, cook for 1 minute, and fill the pot one-third of the way with stock. Bring to a boil, add the tomatoes and oregano to taste, and reduce the heat so that the soup simmers.

4. Scoop the flesh of the butternut squash into a blender and puree until smooth, adding stock as needed.

5. Stir the squash puree, chicken, and quinoa into the simmering broth. Cook until the quinoa is tender, about 15 minutes. Season the soup with salt and pepper and ladle it into warmed bowls.

    As Needed or To Taste: Olive oil, fresh thyme leaves, Chicken Stock (see page 104), cinnamon, salt, pepper

Moroccan Lentil Stew

 +  + +

1½ CUPS BROWN LENTILS   3 CARROTS, PEELED AND CHOPPED   1 LARGE YELLOW ONION, CHOPPED   1 (14 OZ.) CAN OF CANNELLINI BEANS

Directions

1. Place the lentils in a fine sieve and rinse them to remove any impurities. Place them in a slow cooker along with the carrots and onion, fill the slow cooker halfway with stock, and then add garlic, ginger, lemon juice, lemon zest, paprika, cinnamon, coriander, turmeric, cumin, allspice, and bay leaves to taste. Cover and cook on low for 7½ hours.

2. Stir in the cannellini beans, taste the stew, and adjust the seasoning as needed. Cover and cook on low for 30 another minutes. Season with salt and pepper, ladle the stew into warmed bowls, and garnish each portion with fresh mint and goat cheese.

As Needed or To Taste: Vegetable Stock (see page 103), minced garlic, minced fresh ginger, fresh lemon juice, lemon zest, smoked paprika, cinnamon, coriander, turmeric, cumin, allspice, bay leaves, salt, pepper, finely chopped fresh mint, crumbled goat cheese

Avgolemono

 + **+**  **+**

½ CUP ORZO   3 EGGS   1 TABLESPOON FRESH LEMON JUICE   1½ CUPS CHOPPED LEFTOVER CHICKEN

Directions

1. Fill a large saucepan halfway with stock and bring it to a boil. Reduce heat so that the stock simmers, add the orzo, and cook until tender, about 6 minutes.

2. Strain the stock and orzo over a large bowl. Set the orzo aside. Return the stock to the pan and bring it to a simmer.

3. Place the eggs in a mixing bowl and beat until scrambled and frothy. Stir in the lemon juice. While stirring constantly, add approximately ½ cup of the stock to the mixture. Stir another cup of stock into the egg mixture and then stir the tempered eggs into the stock remaining in the pan. Be careful not to let the stock return to a boil.

4. Add the chicken and return the orzo to the soup. Cook, while stirring, until everything is warmed through, about 5 minutes. Season the soup with salt and pepper, ladle into warmed bowls, and garnish each portion with lemon slices and parsley.

As Needed or To Taste: Chicken Stock (see page 104), salt, pepper, lemon slices, finely chopped fresh parsley

Miso Ramen

4 GARLIC CLOVES, MINCED + **2 SHALLOTS, MINCED** + **6 TABLESPOONS WHITE MISO PASTE** + **2 TABLESPOONS SAKE OR RICE VINEGAR**

Directions

1. Coat the bottom of a large saucepan with sesame oil and warm over medium heat. When the oil starts to shimmer, add the garlic and shallots and cook until fragrant, about 2 minutes. Fill the saucepan halfway with stock, stir in the miso and sake or rice vinegar, and add ginger, chili garlic sauce, and brown sugar to taste. Simmer for about 5 minutes and remove the pan from heat. Taste and adjust the seasoning as necessary.

2. Cook the desired amount of ramen noodles according to the manufacturer's instructions. Drain the noodles and place them in warmed bowls. Season the soup with salt and pepper, and ladle the soup over the noodles. Garnish each portion with toasted sesame seeds.

As Needed or To Taste: Sesame oil, minced fresh ginger, chili garlic sauce, brown sugar, Vegetable Stock (see page 103), ramen noodles, salt, pepper, toasted sesame seeds

African Peanut & Quinoa Soup

 **+**  **+**  **+**

| 1 RED ONION, CHOPPED | ½ SWEET POTATO, PEELED AND CHOPPED | 1 ZUCCHINI, CHOPPED | ¾ CUP QUINOA, RINSED |

Directions

1. Coat the bottom of a large saucepan with olive oil and warm it over medium heat. When the oil starts to shimmer, add the red onion, sweet potato, and zucchini and cook until the vegetables are soft, about 10 minutes.

2. Fill the pan halfway with stock, add jalapeño and garlic to taste, and bring the soup to a boil. Reduce the heat so that the soup simmers, stir in the quinoa, season the soup to taste with cumin, cover the pan, and simmer until quinoa is tender, about 15 minutes.

3. Stir in a generous amount of peanut butter, adding a tablespoon at a time until the taste and texture are as desired. Season the soup with salt and pepper, ladle it into warmed bowls, and garnish each portion with oregano and toasted peanuts.

As Needed or To Taste: Olive oil, minced jalapeño pepper, minced garlic, Vegetable Stock (see page 103), cumin, peanut butter, salt, pepper, finely chopped fresh oregano, toasted peanuts

Spring Pea Soup

| 6 STRIPS OF LEMON PEEL | 3 CUPS FRESH PEAS | 3 SHALLOTS, MINCED | 6 FRESH MINT LEAVES, PLUS MORE FOR GARNISH |

Directions

1. Fill a saucepan with water and bring it to a boil. Reduce the heat to medium and add salt along with the strips of lemon peel, peas, and shallots. Cook for 2 to 3 minutes, until the peas are just cooked through. Drain, making sure to reserve 2 cups of the cooking liquid, and immediately transfer the peas, strips of lemon peel, and shallots to a blender. Add the mint leaves and half of the reserved cooking liquid and puree until the desired consistency is achieved, adding more cooking liquid as needed.

2. Place the desired amount of ricotta in a bowl and season it with lemon zest and salt until it has a bright, creamy taste.

3. Season the soup to taste, ladle into warmed bowls, and garnish each portion with a dollop of the lemon ricotta and additional mint.

As Needed or To Taste: Water, ricotta cheese, lemon zest, salt

Pozole

 +  **+** **+**

2 CUPS DRIED HOMINY, SOAKED OVERNIGHT

2 LBS. BONELESS PORK SHOULDER, CUBED

1 LARGE YELLOW ONION, CHOPPED

4 DRIED CHIPOTLE PEPPERS, SEEDED AND CHOPPED

Directions

1. Drain the hominy and set it aside. Coat the bottom of a Dutch oven with olive oil and warm it over medium-high heat. When the oil starts to shimmer, add the pork and onion, season with salt and pepper, and cook, stirring occasionally, until pork and onion are well browned, about 10 minutes.

2. Add the chipotles and hominy, cover the mixture with water, and add cumin and thyme to taste. Bring the soup to a boil, reduce the heat so that it simmers, and cook until the pork and hominy are very tender, about 1½ hours, stirring occasionally.

3. Add the desired amount of garlic, cook for 5 minutes, and taste the soup. Adjust the seasoning as necessary, ladle the soup into warmed bowls, garnish with cilantro, and serve with lime wedges.

As Needed or To Taste: Olive oil, salt, pepper, finely chopped fresh thyme, cumin, minced garlic, finely chopped fresh cilantro, lime wedges

Caldo Verde

 +  + +

| 1 LB. CHORIZO, CHOPPED | 3 YELLOW POTATOES, WASHED AND DICED | ½ WHITE ONION, DICED | 3 CUPS TORN KALE LEAVES |

Directions

1. Place the chorizo, potatoes, and onion in a slow cooker, fill it halfway with stock, and add garlic powder, paprika, salt, and pepper to taste. Cover and cook on high for 3½ hours.

2. Add the kale and cook for another hour. Taste, adjust the seasoning as necessary, and ladle the soup into warmed bowls.

As Needed or To Taste: Chicken Stock (see page 104), garlic powder, paprika, salt, pepper

Black Bean Soup

1 LB. DRIED BLACK BEANS,   1 ONION, CHOPPED
SOAKED OVERNIGHT

Directions

1. Drain the black beans, place them in a slow cooker along with the onion, and add bay leaves, cumin, garlic, and jalapeño to taste. Fill the slow cooker halfway with water and cook on low for 4 hours.

2. Check the beans; if they are not tender, continue cooking on low and check every 15 minutes. If they are tender, season the soup with salt, taste the soup, and adjust the seasoning as needed. Ladle the soup into warmed bowls, garnish each portion with avocado, cilantro, hot sauce, and cheddar cheese, and serve with lime wedges.

As Needed or To Taste: Bay leaves, cumin, minced garlic, water, minced jalapeño pepper, salt, avocado, finely chopped fresh cilantro, hot sauce, cheddar cheese, lime wedges

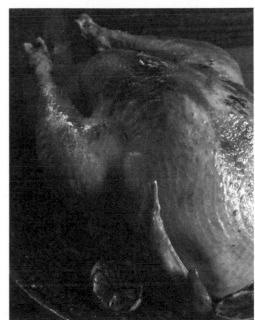

Entrees

Everything that you have learned while preparing the dishes up to this point has been building toward the recipes in this chapter. These are the dishes that will ultimately define your quest to become a better cook, those that you will cap each day with, and use to mark a celebration with loved ones.

Pan-Seared Rib Eye

1 LB. RIB EYE STEAK

+

4 TABLESPOONS UNSALTED BUTTER

+

2 SPRIGS OF FRESH ROSEMARY

Directions

1. Approximately 40 minutes before you are going to start cooking, place the steak on a plate and let it come to room temperature.

2. Coat the bottom of a cast-iron pan with olive oil and warm it over medium-high heat. Pat the steak dry and season it all over with salt. When the oil starts to shimmer, add the steak to the pan and cook until well browned, about 4 minutes. Add 2 tablespoons of the butter to the pan, tilt the pan slightly, and spoon the butter-and-oil mixture over the top of the steak. Repeat this 5 to 6 times as the steak cooks.

3. Cook the steak until it is the desired level of doneness, about 3 more minutes for medium-rare. Transfer the steak to a plate, add the remaining butter and the rosemary to the pan, and spoon the butter-and-oil mixture over the steak. Let the steak rest for 15 minutes before serving.

    As Needed or To Taste: Olive oil, salt

Pulled Pork

 + +

6 TO 8 LB. BONE-IN
PORK SHOULDER

¼ CUP BROWN SUGAR

1 LARGE ONION,
CHOPPED

Directions

1. Preheat the oven to 300°F. Season the pork shoulder with salt and let it rest at room temperature. Coat the bottom of a Dutch oven with olive oil and warm It over medium heat. When the oil starts to shimmer, add the pork shoulder and cook, turning occasionally, until it is browned all over, about 8 minutes. Remove the pan from heat.

2. Add the brown sugar and onion to the pot, fill it halfway with stock, and add peppercorns, mustard, paprika, and bay leaves to taste. Cover the Dutch oven, place it in the oven, and braise until the meat is very tender, about 4 hours. Remove from the oven, shred the meat with a fork, and serve.

As Needed or To Taste: Salt, olive oil, Chicken Stock (see page 104), whole peppercorns, mustard, paprika, bay leaves

Perfect Prime Rib

 +  +

**6 LB. PRIME RIB
(4-BONE ROAST)**   **1 STICK OF
UNSALTED BUTTER**   **10 GARLIC CLOVES,
MINCED**

Directions

1. Let the prime rib stand at room temperature for 2 to 3 hours before you cook it.

2. Preheat the oven to 480°F and pat the prime rib dry with a paper towel. Place the butter in a saucepan and melt it over medium heat. Add the garlic, season it with salt, and sauté until the garlic is fragrant, about 1 minute. Pour the mixture into a bowl and let it cool slightly.

3. Place the prime rib in a roasting pan and rub the garlic butter all over it. Place the prime rib in the oven and roast until it has browned, 20 to 25 minutes. Reduce the oven's temperature to 250°F and cover the roast with aluminum foil. Roast until the internal temperature of the prime rib is 118°F. Remove from the oven and let it rest for 20 minutes, which allows the prime rib's internal temperature to rise to 125°F, which is medium-rare. Slice and serve.

As Needed or To Taste: Salt

Thanksgiving Turkey

 **+**  **+**  **+**

| 1 ONION, HALVED | 1 LEMON, HALVED | 10 TO 20 LB. TURKEY, GIBLETS REMOVED AND RINSED | 5 TABLESPOONS UNSALTED BUTTER |

Directions

1. Preheat the oven to 450°F. Warm a cast-iron skillet over high heat. Place the onion and lemon in the pan, cut side down, and sear until they are dark brown. Remove from the pan and set aside.

2. Pat the turkey dry. Place the onion and lemon in the cavity of the bird and add sage leaves to taste. Slice a small slit in the skin of the breast, being careful not to puncture the meat. Using your index finger, carefully separate the skin from the meat. Once you have separated the skin, spread the butter in between the skin and meat. Season the turkey generously with salt, place it in a roasting pan, and cover the pan with a lid or aluminum foil.

3. Place the turkey in the oven and roast for 30 minutes. Reduce the oven's temperature to 350°F and roast until a meat thermometer registers 155°F when inserted into the breast, 2½ to 4½ hours depending on the size of the turkey. Remove from the oven and let the turkey rest for 20 minutes before slicing and serving.

As Needed or To Taste: Fresh sage leaves, salt

Spaghetti alla Carbonara

 + +  +

4 OZ. BACON   2 LARGE EGGS, AT ROOM TEMPERATURE   ¾ CUP GRATED PARMESAN CHEESE, PLUS MORE FOR GARNISH   1 LB. SPAGHETTI

Directions

1. Bring a large saucepan of water to a boil. Coat the bottom of a skillet with olive oil and warm it over medium heat. When the oil starts to shimmer, add the bacon, season it with pepper, and cook, stirring occasionally, until the fat renders and it starts turning golden brown, about 6 minutes. Remove the skillet from heat and partially cover it.

2. Place the eggs in a small bowl and whisk until scrambled. Stir in the Parmesan and season the mixture with salt and pepper.

3. Add salt and the pasta to the boiling water. Cook 2 minutes short of the directed cooking time, so that the pasta is soft but still very firm. Reserve ¼ cup of the pasta water and drain the pasta. Return the pot to the stove, raise the heat to high, and add a dash of olive oil and the reserved pasta water. Add the drained pasta and toss until it has absorbed the water. Remove the pot from heat, stir in the bacon and the egg-and-Parmesan mixture, and toss to coat the pasta. Divide the pasta between four warm bowls, season with pepper, and top each portion with additional Parmesan.

As Needed or To Taste: Olive oil, pepper, salt

Spicy Sausage & Peppers

 +  +

5 BELL PEPPERS, STEMMED, SEEDS AND RIBS REMOVED, AND SLICED

1 (28 OZ.) CAN OF FIRE-ROASTED TOMATOES

2 LBS. KIELBASA, CUT INTO 6 PIECES

Directions

1. Place the bell peppers in a slow cooker and set it to high heat. Place the tomatoes in a blender, add garlic, chipotles in adobo, and adobo sauce to taste, and puree until smooth. Pour the puree over the peppers and stir to combine. Add the kielbasa to the slow cooker, cover, and cook on high for 4 hours.

2. To serve, ladle the preparation into warmed bowls or submarine rolls.

As needed or To Taste: Minced garlic, chipotle peppers in adobo, adobo sauce, submarine rolls

Spicy Tonkatsu

 + **+** **+**

1½ LBS. PORK CUTLETS   ¼ CUP WASABI PASTE   2 TABLESPOONS HORSERADISH   2 CUPS PANKO

Directions

1. Pat the cutlets dry and lightly coat each one with some of the wasabi paste. Place the horseradish in a bowl and add olive oil, parsley, chives, salt, and pepper to taste. Add the panko and carefully stir to combine. Set the seasoned panko aside.

2. Coat the bottom of a large cast-iron skillet with olive oil and warm it over medium heat. When the oil starts to shimmer, add the pork cutlets and cook until golden brown, about 4 minutes. Flip the cutlets over and cook until golden brown on the other side, another 4 minutes.

3. Set the broiler on your oven to high. Remove the cutlets from the skillet and dip each one into the seasoned panko until completely coated. Return the coated cutlets to the skillet. While keeping a close watch, place the pan under the broiler. Broil, turning the cutlets over once, until the crust is browned and crispy. Slice thin and serve with lemon wedges.

As Needed or To Taste: Olive oil, finely chopped fresh parsley, finely chopped fresh chives, salt, pepper, lemon wedges

Teriyaki Sauce

Place 1 tablespoon minced ginger, 3 minced garlic cloves, 1 tablespoon rice vinegar, 2 tablespoons brown sugar, ¼ cup soy sauce, 1 tablespoon cornstarch, and ½ cup water in a blender and puree until smooth. Transfer to a saucepan and cook, stirring frequently, over medium heat until the sauce starts to thicken, about 6 minutes.

Teriyaki Salmon with Vegetables

4 CHINESE EGGPLANTS, SLICED

+

1 RED BELL PEPPER, STEMMED, SEEDS AND RIBS REMOVED, AND SLICED THIN

+

1 CUP BEAN SPROUTS

+

4 SALMON FILLETS, BONED

Directions

1. Preheat the oven to 375°F. Coat the bottom of a large cast-iron skillet with olive oil and warm it over medium-high heat. When the oil starts to shimmer, add the eggplants and bell pepper along with scallions to taste and sauté until the eggplants start to collapse, about 5 minutes.

2. Stir in the bean sprouts and place the salmon on top of the vegetables, skin side down. Season with salt, pepper, and some of the Teriyaki Sauce and transfer the pan to the oven. Bake until the salmon is cooked through, about 8 minutes, and remove the pan from the oven. Serve with the remaining Teriyaki Sauce.

As Needed or To Taste: Olive oil, chopped scallions, salt, pepper, Teriyaki Sauce (see sidebar)

Baked Cod with Lemons, Capers & Leeks

| ½ LB. LEEKS, TRIMMED AND RINSED WELL | 1½ LBS. COD FILLETS | 3 TABLESPOONS CAPERS | ½ LEMON, SLICED THIN |

Directions

1. Preheat the oven to 400°F. Pat the leeks dry, place them in a baking dish, and season with salt and pepper. Place the leeks in the oven and roast until they start to brown, about 25 minutes.

2. Remove the leeks from the oven, place the cod fillets on top of them, and sprinkle lemon juice over the fish. Distribute the capers and slices of lemon over the cod fillets and place the baking dish back in the oven. Roast until the cod is cooked through and can be flaked with a fork, about 25 minutes. Serve with lemon wedges.

As Needed or To Taste: Salt, pepper, olive oil, fresh lemon juice, lemon wedges

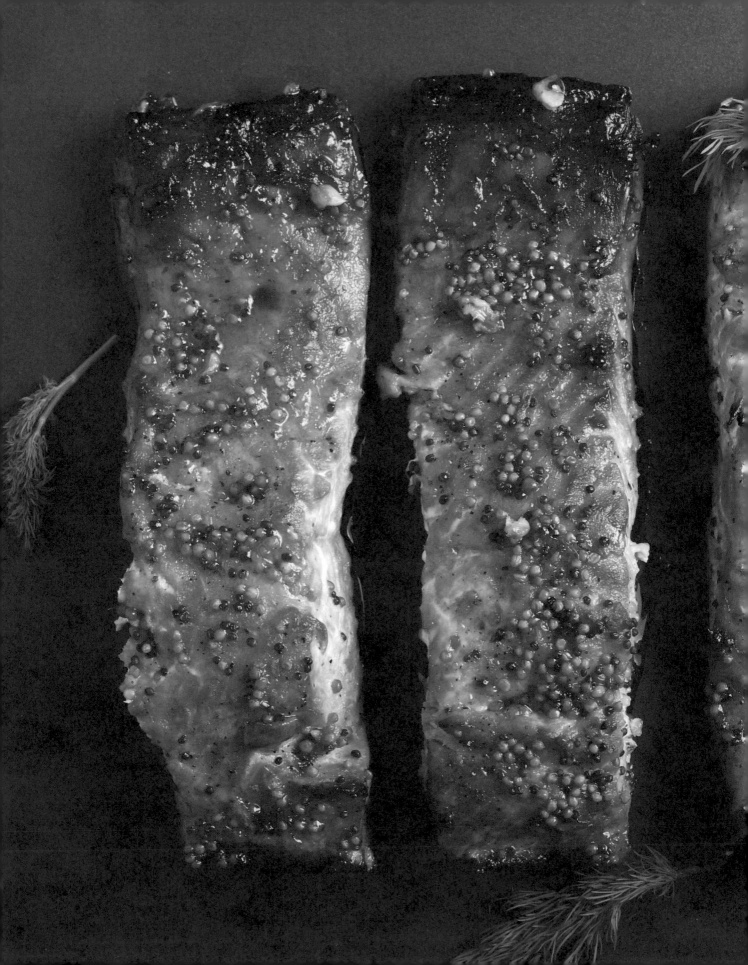

Honey Mustard Salmon

 **+** **+** **+**

1½ LBS. SALMON FILLETS, BONED	2 TABLESPOONS WHOLE-GRAIN MUSTARD	1 TABLESPOON HONEY	2 GARLIC CLOVES, MINCED

Directions

1. Preheat the oven to 375°F. Season the salmon fillets with salt and let them rest at room temperature for 15 minutes.

2. Place the mustard, honey, and garlic in a mixing bowl, add olive oil, smoked paprika, and pepper to taste, and stir to combine. Place the salmon in a baking dish and brush the honey mustard mixture over the tops of the fillets. Cover the dish with foil, place it in the oven, and bake the salmon for 15 minutes.

3. Remove the foil and set the oven's broiler to high. Broil the salmon until the tops of the fillets are browned and crispy, 2 to 3 minutes. Remove from the oven and serve with lemon wedges.

As Needed or To Taste: Salt, olive oil, smoked paprika, pepper, lemon wedges

Bacon Cheeseburgers

 + + +

1 LB. GROUND BEEF   1 EGG   ⅓ CUP BREAD CRUMBS   8 SLICES OF THICK-CUT BACON, COOKED

Directions

1. Preheat your outdoor grill to medium-high heat (about 450°F) or warm a cast-iron skillet on the stove. Place the ground beef, egg, and bread crumbs in a bowl, season the mixture with salt and pepper, and stir to combine.

2. Divide the mixture into four balls and press down on them to form each one into a 1-inch-thick patty. Place the burgers on the grill or in the pan. Cover and cook for 5 minutes.

3. Flip the patties over, cover, and cook until cooked through, about 5 minutes. When the burgers have about 1 minute left to cook, place slices of cheese on them. When the burgers are cooked and the cheese has melted, top each burger with some of the bacon and serve with hamburger buns. Place cooked bacon on top of the burger and serve.

As Needed or To Taste: Salt, pepper, slices of cheese, hamburger buns

American Chop Suey

1 LB. ELBOW MACARONI

\+

1 LB. GROUND BEEF

\+

1 ONION, DICED

\+

1 (14 OZ.) CAN OF DICED TOMATOES

Directions

1. Bring water to a boil in a large saucepan. Add salt and the macaroni and cook until the macaroni is just shy of al dente, about 7 minutes. Drain and set aside.

2. While the water for the macaroni is coming to a boil, place the beef in a large skillet, season it with salt and pepper, and cook over medium-high heat, breaking the beef up with a fork, until it starts to brown, about 5 minutes. Stir in the onion and sauté until the beef is cooked through and the onion is translucent, about 3 minutes. Add the tomatoes and cook for about 3 minutes, stirring frequently.

3. Stir the macaroni into the skillet and cook until everything is warmed through. Season with salt and pepper and serve.

As Needed or To Taste: Salt, pepper

Tuscan Chicken

 + +  +

4 BONELESS, SKINLESS CHICKEN BREASTS	6 GARLIC CLOVES, MINCED	3 CUPS BABY SPINACH	½ CUP GRATED PARMESAN CHEESE

Directions

1. Pat the chicken dry with paper towels and season it with salt, pepper, and paprika. Coat the bottom of a large skillet with olive oil and warm it over medium-high heat. When the oil starts to shimmer, add the chicken and cook until golden brown on each side and cooked through, about 6 minutes per side. Remove the chicken from the pan and set it aside.

2. Add the garlic to the pan and sauté until it is fragrant, about 1 minute. Stir in a generous amount of sun-dried tomatoes and sauté for another 4 minutes.

3. Deglaze the pan with heavy cream, add mustard to taste, and bring the cream to a gentle simmer. Add the spinach, cook until it wilts, about 2 minutes, and then stir in the Parmesan. Return the chicken to the pan and cook until warmed through. Garnish with parsley before serving.

   As Needed or To Taste: Salt, pepper, paprika, olive oil, sun-dried tomatoes in olive oil, heavy cream, Dijon mustard, finely chopped fresh parsley

Pesto Chicken with Charred Tomatoes

 + +

2 LBS. CHICKEN PIECES   2 BATCHES OF BASIL PESTO   4 PLUM TOMATOES, HALVED
                                        (SEE PAGE 73)

Directions

1. Season the chicken with salt and pepper. Place the pesto in a bowl, add the chicken pieces, and stir until they are evenly coated. Cover the bowl and let the chicken marinate in the refrigerator for 2 hours.

2. Preheat the oven to 400°F. Remove the chicken from the refrigerator and let it come to room temperature.

3. Place the chicken in a baking dish. Season the tomatoes with salt and pepper and place them in the baking dish. Cover the dish with aluminum foil, place it in the oven, and roast for 25 minutes. Remove the foil and continue roasting until the chicken is cooked through, about 25 minutes. Remove from the oven and let the chicken rest for 10 minutes before serving.

As Needed or To Taste: Salt, pepper

Veal Scallopini

 +  +

1 LB. VEAL CUTLETS,
POUNDED THIN

¼ CUP PITTED AND
SLICED GREEN OLIVES

ZEST AND JUICE
OF 1 LEMON

Directions

1. Warm a large cast-iron skillet over medium heat for 5 minutes. Place flour in a shallow bowl, add nutmeg, salt, and pepper to taste, and stir to combine.

2. Coat the bottom of the pan with butter. When it starts to sizzle, dredge the veal in the seasoned flour until lightly coated on both sides. Working in batches, place the veal in the skillet and cook for about 1 minute on each side, until browned and the juices run clear. Set the cooked veal aside.

3. Deglaze the pan with stock, scraping any browned bits up from the bottom. Add the olives, lemon zest, and lemon juice, stir to combine, and cook until the desired texture is achieved. To serve, plate the veal and pour the pan sauce over each cutlet.

As Needed or To Taste: All-purpose flour, freshly grated nutmeg, salt, pepper, unsalted butter, Beef Stock (see page 106)

Veggie Burgers

 + + +

1 (14 OZ.) CAN OF BLACK BEANS, DRAINED AND RINSED   ¼ CUP CORN KERNELS   ½ CUP PANKO   1 EGG, LIGHTLY BEATEN

Directions

1. Place half of the beans in a food processor, add scallions and roasted red peppers to taste, and pulse until the mixture is a thick paste. Transfer it to a large bowl.

2. Stir the corn, panko, and egg into the paste, add cilantro, cumin, cayenne, pepper, and lime juice to taste, and then incorporate the remaining beans. Stir until the mixture holds together. Form the mixture into four patties.

3. Coat the bottom of a large skillet with olive oil and warm it over medium-high heat. When the oil starts to shimmer, add the patties, cover the skillet, and cook until browned and cooked through, about 5 minutes per side. Serve on hamburger buns or over arugula.

As Needed or To Taste: Chopped roasted red peppers, minced scallion, finely chopped fresh cilantro, cumin, cayenne, pepper, fresh lime juice, olive oil, hamburger buns, arugula

Saag Aloo

½ LB. FINGERLING OR
RED POTATOES, CHOPPED

\+

1 ONION, CHOPPED

\+

1 LB. FROZEN
CHOPPED SPINACH

Directions

1. Coat the bottom of a large skillet with olive oil and warm it over medium heat. When the oil starts to shimmer, add the potatoes and cook until they start to brown, about 5 minutes.

2. Add the onion and sauté until it starts to soften, about 5 minutes. Add mustard seeds, cumin, garlic, and ginger to taste and cook, stirring constantly, until the mixture is very fragrant, about 2 minutes.

3. Stir in the frozen spinach, season the mixture with red pepper flakes, and cover the pan with a lid. Cook, stirring occasionally, until the spinach has thawed and is warmed through, about 10 minutes. Add water to the pan if the mixture looks dry.

4. Remove the cover and cook all of the liquid has evaporated. Season the saag aloo with salt, add yogurt until you have the desired level of creaminess, and serve.

   As Needed or To Taste: Olive oil, mustard seeds, cumin, minced garlic, minced ginger, red pepper flakes, salt, plain yogurt

Lemon & Garlic Shrimp

 +  +

4 TABLESPOONS
UNSALTED BUTTER, AT
ROOM TEMPERATURE

1 LB. SHRIMP, PEELED
AND DEVEINED

8 GARLIC CLOVES,
MINCED

Directions

1. Place a large cast-iron skillet over medium heat and add the butter. When the butter has melted and is foaming, add the shrimp and cook, without stirring, for 2 minutes. Remove the shrimp from the pan with a slotted spoon and set them aside.

2. Reduce the heat to medium-low, add the garlic to the pan, and season it generously with lemon-pepper seasoning. Cook until the garlic has started to brown, about 1 minute. Return the shrimp to the pan and cook until warmed through, about 1 minute. To serve, sprinkle lemon juice over the dish and garnish with parsley.

As Needed or To Taste: Lemon-pepper seasoning, fresh lemon juice, finely chopped fresh parsley

Shredded Chicken with Beans & Rice

 +  +  +

2 LBS. BONELESS, SKINLESS CHICKEN BREASTS

1 CUP WHITE RICE

2 PLUM TOMATOES, CHOPPED

1 (14 OZ.) CAN OF BLACK BEANS, DRAINED AND RINSED

Directions

1. Place the chicken in a slow cooker, cover it with stock, and add jalapeño, garlic, cumin, and garlic powder to taste. Cook on high until the chicken is very tender and falling apart, about 4 hours. Remove the chicken from the slow cooker, place it in a bowl, and shred it with a fork. Cover the bowl with aluminum foil and set it aside.

2. Add the rice and tomatoes to the slow cooker, season the mixture with salt and pepper, and cook until the rice is tender, 40 to 50 minutes. Make sure to check on the rice after 30 minutes, since cook times will vary between different brands of slow cookers.

3. Add the black beans to the slow cooker, stir to combine, top with the shredded chicken, and cover the slow cooker until everything is warmed through. Garnish with additional jalapeño and serve.

   As Needed or To Taste: Chicken Stock (see page 104), minced jalapeño pepper, minced garlic, cumin, garlic powder, salt, pepper

Pork Fried Rice

  +  +   +

| 3 LARGE EGGS | 2 CARROTS, PEELED AND MINCED | 4 CUPS DAY-OLD WHITE RICE | 2 CUPS CHOPPED LEFTOVER PORK TENDERLOIN |

Directions

1. Coat the bottom of a large skillet with olive oil and warm it over medium-high heat. When the oil starts to shimmer, add ginger and garlic and sauté until fragrant, about 1 minute.

2. Add the eggs and scramble until they are set, about 2 minutes. Stir in the carrots, rice, and pork, add scallions, peas, soy sauce, rice vinegar, fish sauce, and sesame oil to taste, and cook, stirring constantly, until the pork is warmed through, about 5 minutes.

As Needed or To Taste: Olive oil, minced ginger, minced garlic, chopped scallions, frozen peas, soy sauce, rice vinegar, fish sauce, sesame oil

Fish & Chips

 **+** **+** **+**

5 POTATOES, SLICED INTO LONG, THIN STRIPS   2 EGGS, BEATEN   1 CUP CORNMEAL   1½ LBS. POLLOCK FILLETS

Directions

1. Add canola oil to a Dutch oven until it is 2 inches deep and warm it to 350°F over medium-high heat. Place the potatoes in the oil and fry until golden brown. Remove the fried potatoes with a slotted spoon and transfer to a paper towel–lined plate to drain. Warm the oil back to 350°F. When the potatoes have drained, place them in a bowl, add rosemary and salt to taste, and toss to coat.

2. Place the beaten eggs in a small bowl and the cornmeal in another. Dip the pollock fillets in the egg and then in the cornmeal, repeating until they are coated all over. Place the battered pollock in the oil and fry until golden brown and cooked through, 5 to 7 minutes. Remove and set to drain and cool on another paper towel–lined plate. When all of the pollock has been cooked, serve with the fried potatoes and lemon wedges.

As Needed or To Taste: Canola oil, finely chopped fresh rosemary, salt, lemon wedges

Steak with Peppers & Onions

 +  + +

2 LBS. SIRLOIN TIPS, SLICED

1 TABLESPOON MUSTARD POWDER

2 YELLOW ONIONS, CHOPPED

2 RED BELL PEPPERS, STEMMED, SEEDS AND RIBS REMOVED, AND CHOPPED

Directions

1. Place the sirloin tips in a mixing bowl, sprinkle the mustard powder over them, and add olive oil, garlic, Worcestershire sauce, and red wine vinegar to taste. Stir to combine, cover the bowl, and marinate the sirloin tips in the refrigerator for 2 hours.

2. Approximately 30 minutes before you are ready to cook, remove the sirloin tips from the marinade and allow them to come to room temperature.

3. Coat the bottom of a large cast-iron skillet with olive oil and warm it over medium-high heat. When it starts to shimmer, add the sirloin tips and cook, stirring occasionally, until they are browned all over, about 8 minutes. Remove the sirloin tips from the pan and set them aside.

4. Reduce the heat to medium, add the onions and peppers, and cook, without stirring, until they are starting to brown, about 8 minutes. Return the sirloin tips to the pan and cook for an additional 2 minutes. Season with salt and pepper and serve immediately.

As Needed or To Taste: Olive oil, minced garlic, Worcestershire sauce, red wine vinegar, salt, pepper

New York-Style Pizza

 **+** **+**  **+**

⅛ TEASPOON
INSTANT YEAST

6.75 OZ. WATER

10.9 OZ. BREAD FLOUR
OR "00" FLOUR, PLUS
MORE AS NEEDED

1½ TEASPOONS
TABLE SALT

Directions

1. In a large bowl, combine the yeast, flour, and water. Work the mixture until it just holds together. Dust a work surface with either bread or "00" flour and knead the dough until it is compact, smooth, and elastic.

2. Add the salt and knead until the dough is developed and elastic, meaning it pulls back when stretched. Transfer the dough to an airtight container and let it rest at room temperature for 2 hours.

3. Divide the dough into two pieces and shape them into very tight balls. Place the balls of dough in a baking dish with high edges, leaving enough space between rounds that they won't touch when fully risen. Cover with oiled plastic wrap and let them rest until they have doubled in size, about 6 hours.

4. Place a baking stone on the middle rack of your oven and preheat the oven to the maximum temperature. Dust a work surface with semolina flour, place the balls of dough on the surface, and gently stretch them into 10- to 12-inch rounds. Cover them with sauce and top with the mozzarella. Season with oregano and drizzle olive oil over the pizzas.

5. Using a peel or a flat baking sheet, transfer one pizza at a time to the heated baking stone in the oven. Bake for about 15 minutes, until the crust is golden brown and starting to char. Remove, repeat with the other pizza, and let both cool slightly before serving.

As Needed or To Taste: Olive oil, semolina flour, marinara sauce, shredded mozzarella cheese, dried oregano

Bulgogi

 + +  +

| 2 LBS. PORK TENDERLOIN, SLICED THIN | 4 GARLIC CLOVES, MINCED | 1-INCH PIECE OF FRESH GINGER, PEELED AND MINCED | ½ CUP GOCHUJANG (KOREAN CHILI PASTE) |

Directions

1. Place the pork, garlic, ginger, and gochujang in a mixing bowl, add soy sauce and sesame oil to taste, and stir to combine. Place the bowl in the refrigerator and let the pork marinate for 30 minutes.

2. Warm a 12-inch cast-iron skillet over high heat for 5 minutes. When it is extremely hot, add the marinated pork and sear, turning the pork as it browns, until it is cooked through, about 5 minutes.

3. Garnish with the sesame seeds and scallions.

As Needed or To Taste: Soy sauce, sesame oil, sesame seeds, chopped scallions

Fried Chicken

 **+** **+**  **+**

| 6 BONE-IN, SKIN-ON CHICKEN PIECES | 2 EGGS, LIGHTLY BEATEN | 1½ CUPS CORNFLAKES, FINELY CRUSHED | ½ CUP BREAD CRUMBS |

Directions

1. Preheat the oven to 400°F and place a cast-iron skillet in the oven as it warms. To begin preparations for the chicken, rinse the chicken pieces under cold water and pat them dry. Place flour in a shallow bowl, add salt and pepper, and stir to combine. Place milk and vinegar in another bowl and let the mixture sit for 10 minutes.

2. Stir the eggs into the milk mixture. In another large bowl, combine the cornflakes and bread crumbs and season the mixture with paprika. Dip the chicken pieces into the seasoned flour, then the milk mixture, then the bread crumb mixture, repeating until the pieces are completely coated. Put the pieces on a plate, cover with plastic wrap, and refrigerate for about 15 minutes.

3. Put on oven mitts, remove the skillet from the oven, and place about 1 inch of vegetable oil in it. Warm the oil over medium heat until it is 350°F. Place the cold chicken pieces in the skillet and turn them in the hot oil until both sides are browned. Put the skillet in the oven and bake for about 30 minutes, turning the pieces over halfway through. The chicken is done when the juices run clear when pierced with a fork. Remove from the oven and serve.

As Needed or To Taste: All-purpose flour, salt, pepper, milk, white vinegar, paprika, vegetable oil

Lamb & Peas Curry

 **+**  **+**

1 ONION, CHOPPED   1 LB. GROUND LAMB   ½ CUP CHOPPED TOMATOES   1 CUP FROZEN PEAS

Directions

1. Coat the bottom of a large skillet with olive oil and warm it over medium-high heat. When the oil starts to shimmer, add the onion and sauté until it starts to brown, about 10 minutes.

2. Add garlic and ginger to the pan, sauté for 2 minutes, and then add the lamb, using a fork to break it up as it browns. Cook the lamb until fully browned, about 8 minutes.

3. Season the mixture with curry powder, cook for 1 minute, stir in the tomatoes, and cook until they start to collapse, about 5 minutes. Add the frozen peas and stir until they are warmed through. Season the dish with salt, add yogurt until you have the desired level of creaminess, and, if desired, serve over jasmine rice.

As Needed or To Taste: Olive oil, minced garlic, grated ginger, curry powder, salt, plain yogurt, cooked jasmine rice

Cottage Pie

 +  + +

6 RUSSET POTATOES, PEELED AND CHOPPED

1 STICK OF UNSALTED BUTTER, DIVIDED INTO TABLESPOONS

½ YELLOW ONION, MINCED

1 LB. GROUND BEEF

Directions

1. Preheat the oven to 350°F. Place the potatoes in a large saucepan and cover with water. Bring the water to a boil, add salt, and reduce the heat so that the water simmers. Cook the potatoes until they are fork-tender, about 20 minutes. Drain the potatoes and place them in a large bowl. Add 6 tablespoons of the butter and mash the potatoes until they are smooth and creamy, adding milk and yogurt as needed to get the desired texture. Season the mashed potatoes with salt and pepper and set them aside.

2. Coat the bottom of a large cast-iron skillet with olive oil and warm it over medium heat. When the oil starts to shimmer, add the onion and sauté until translucent, about 3 minutes. Add the ground beef and cook, while breaking it up with a fork, until browned, about 8 minutes. Drain the fat from the skillet, stir in the preferred amount of peas and corn, and season the mixture with salt and pepper.

3. Spread the mashed potatoes over the meat and vegetables and use a rubber spatula to smooth the top. Cut the remaining butter into slivers and dot the potatoes with them. Cover the skillet with aluminum foil, place it in the oven, and bake for 30 minutes. Remove the foil and bake for another 10 minutes, until the potatoes start to turn golden brown. Remove the cottage pie from the oven and let cool for 5 minutes before serving.

As Needed or To Taste: Salt, milk, plain yogurt, pepper, olive oil, frozen peas, corn kernels

Pad Thai

 + +  +

3 BONELESS, SKINLESS CHICKEN BREASTS   1 LARGE EGG   ¼ CUP TAMARIND PASTE   1 CUP BEAN SPROUTS

Directions

1. Place the desired amount of noodles in a baking dish and cover them with boiling water. Stir and let stand until they are tender, about 15 minutes.

2. Coat a large wok or skillet with olive oil and warm it over medium-high heat. When the oil starts to shimmer, add the chicken and cook until it is browned on both sides and springy to the touch, about 8 minutes. Remove the chicken from the pan and let it cool briefly. When cool enough to handle, slice the chicken into thin strips.

3. Add the noodles and the egg to the pan and cook until the egg is set. Stir in the tamarind paste and bean sprouts and add fish sauce, rice vinegar, brown sugar, scallions, and cayenne to taste. Return the chicken to the pan and cook until everything is warmed through. Sprinkle crushed peanuts over the dish and serve with lime wedges.

    As Needed or To Taste: Rice noodles, olive oil, fish sauce, rice vinegar, brown sugar, chopped scallions, cayenne pepper, crushed peanuts, lime wedges

Coconut Chicken Curry

 + +  +

6 BONELESS, SKINLESS CHICKEN THIGHS   **2 YELLOW ONIONS, SLICED**   **2 RED BELL PEPPERS, STEMMED, SEEDS AND RIBS REMOVED, AND SLICED**   **1 (14 OZ.) CAN OF COCONUT MILK**

Directions

1. Rub the chicken thighs with green curry paste and let them rest at room temperature for 30 minutes.

2. Coat the bottom of a large cast-iron skillet with olive oil and warm it over medium-high heat. When the oil starts to shimmer, add the chicken and cook until browned on both sides, about 3 minutes per side. Remove the chicken from the skillet and set it aside.

3. Add the onions and peppers and sauté until they have softened, about 5 minutes. Add garlic, ginger, and green curry paste to taste and cook until the mixture is very fragrant, about 2 minutes.

4. Add the coconut milk and scrape up any browned bits from the bottom of the pan. Season the mixture with fish sauce and curry powder and add Thai basil to taste. Return the chicken to the pan, cover the skillet, and cook until the chicken is cooked through and tender, about 10 minutes. Garnish with cilantro and additional Thai basil and serve with lime wedges.

As Needed or To Taste: Green curry paste, olive oil, minced ginger, minced garlic, fish sauce, curry powder, finely chopped fresh Thai basil, finely chopped fresh cilantro, lime wedges

Green Bean & Tofu Casserole

 +  +

1 LB. EXTRA-FIRM TOFU, DRAINED AND CHOPPED   1 LB. GREEN BEANS   4 OZ. SHIITAKE MUSHROOMS, SLICED

Directions

1. Place the tofu in a mixing bowl, add soy sauce, rice vinegar, sesame oil, honey, cinnamon, and pepper to taste, and fold the mixture until the tofu is coated. Cover the bowl, place it in the refrigerator, and let it marinate for 2 days, gently stirring occasionally.

2. Preheat the oven to 375°F. Remove the cubes of tofu from the bag. Place the green beans and mushrooms in the bag and shake until the vegetables are coated. Line a 9 x 13–inch baking pan with parchment paper and place the tofu on it in an even layer. Place in the oven and roast for 35 minutes. Remove the pan, flip the cubes of tofu over, and push them to the edge of the pan. Add the green bean-and-mushroom mixture, return the pan to the oven, and roast for 15 minutes, or until the green beans are cooked to your preference. Remove the pan from the oven, garnish with the sesame seeds, and serve.

As Needed or To Taste: Soy sauce, rice vinegar, sesame oil, honey, cinnamon, pepper, sesame seeds

Goulash

 **+**   **+**  **+**

| 3 LBS. BEEF CHUCK, TRIMMED | 3 YELLOW ONIONS, CHOPPED | 2 BELL PEPPERS, STEMMED, SEEDS AND RIBS REMOVED, AND CHOPPED | 3 TABLESPOONS SWEET HUNGARIAN PAPRIKA |

Directions

1. Coat the bottom of a Dutch oven with olive oil and warm it over medium heat. When the oil starts to shimmer, add the meat in batches and cook until it is browned all over, taking care not to crowd the pot. Remove the browned beef and set it aside.

2. Reduce the heat to medium-low. Let the pot cool for 2 minutes and then add the onions and peppers. Stir to coat with the pan drippings and sauté the vegetables until they are browned, about 10 minutes. Add caraway seeds to taste and cook until they are fragrant, about 1 minute.

3. Cover the mixture with flour, sprinkle the paprika over it, and add tomato paste, garlic, brown sugar, salt, and pepper to taste. Stir to combine and then fill the pot one-third of the way with stock, scraping up any browned bits from the bottom.

4. Bring the goulash to a boil, reduce the heat, and let it simmer until it thickens slightly, about 10 minutes. Return the meat to the Dutch oven, cover, and simmer over low heat until the meat is very tender, about 2 hours. To serve, stir in sour cream to taste, and serve over cooked egg noodles.

As Needed or To Taste: Olive oil, caraway seeds, all-purpose flour, tomato paste, minced garlic, brown sugar, Beef Stock (see page 106), sour cream, cooked egg noodles

Roasted Chicken

3 TO 4 LB. CHICKEN

Directions

1. Preheat the oven to 450°F and place a cast-iron skillet in the oven as it warms. Rinse the chicken, inside and outside, and pat it dry with paper towels. This step is important because it ensures that the chicken will roast rather than steam.

2. Season with chicken generously, inside and outside, with salt and pepper. Put on oven mitts, remove the skillet from the oven, and place the chicken, breast-side down, in the pan.

3. Place the pan in the oven and roast for 20 minutes. Reduce the oven's temperature to 350°F and roast until a meat thermometer inserted in the breast registers 165°F, about 35 minutes. Remove from the oven, baste the chicken with the pan juices, and let it rest for 15 minutes before carving and serving.

As Needed or To Taste: Salt, pepper

Chicken with 40 Cloves

 **+**  **+** **+**

| 3 BONELESS, SKINLESS CHICKEN BREASTS | 8 WHITE MUSHROOMS, QUARTERED | 40 GARLIC CLOVES | ⅓ CUP DRY VERMOUTH |

Directions

1. Preheat the oven to 350°F. Generously season the chicken with salt and pepper and put a Dutch oven over high heat. Add the chicken in one layer, cooking in batches if necessary. Although oil is not necessarily needed when cooking chicken thighs, if the pan looks dry add a drizzle of olive oil. When brown on one side, flip to the other side and repeat. Transfer the chicken thighs to a plate when fully browned but before they are cooked through.

2. Put the mushrooms in the pot and sauté over medium heat, stirring occasionally, until they are browned all over, about 10 minutes. Add the garlic and sauté for 1 minute. Deglaze the pot with the vermouth, scraping the browned bits up from the bottom. Return the chicken thighs to the pot and add stock until the liquid is almost covering them.

3. Cover the Dutch oven, place the pot in the oven, and braise the chicken until tender and cooked through, about 25 minutes.

4. Remove from the oven and transfer the chicken and mushrooms to a separate plate. With a wooden spoon, mash about half of the garlic cloves and stir to incorporate them into the pan sauce. If the sauce is still thin, place the pot over medium-high heat and cook until it has reduced. Return the chicken and mushrooms to the pot, reduce the heat, and cook until warmed through. Add the butter ½ tablespoon at a time until the taste and texture are to your liking. Garnish each portion with a sprinkling of tarragon.

As Needed or To Taste: Salt, pepper, olive oil, Chicken Stock (see page 104), unsalted butter, finely chopped fresh tarragon

Crispy Pork Belly with Balsamic Glaze

 +  +

2 LBS. PORK BELLY, SKIN ON   1 CUP BALSAMIC VINEGAR   ¼ CUP BROWN SUGAR

Directions

1. Rub a generous amount of salt over the pork belly. Place a wire rack in a rimmed baking sheet, place the pork belly on it, and refrigerate overnight.

2. Preheat the oven to 300°F. Bring water to a boil and remove the pork belly from the refrigerator. Pour the boiling water over the pork belly's skin. Let it cool and drain. Pat the pork belly's skin dry with paper towels, place it in a baking dish, and season generously with salt. Place in the oven and roast for 3 hours.

3. Remove the pork belly from the oven and raise the temperature to 500°F. When the oven is ready, place the pork belly back in the oven and cook until the skin is puffy and crisp, about 10 minutes. Remove from the oven and transfer the pork belly to a cutting board.

4. Place the balsamic vinegar and sugar in a saucepan and bring it to a gentle boil. Reduce the heat to medium-low and simmer for 8 to 10 minutes, stirring often, until the mixture thickens. Remove the pan from heat and let it cool for 15 minutes. To serve, slice the pork belly and drizzle with the glaze.

As Needed or To Taste: Salt

Bone-In Pork Roast

7 TO 8-BONE, CENTER-CUT
RACK OF PORK

¼ CUP DIJON MUSTARD

Directions

1. Preheat the oven to 450°F. Rinse the rack of pork under cold water and pat dry with paper towels. Place the rack fat side up in a roasting pan.

2. In a bowl, combine all of the spices and mix well. Rub the mustard into the top of the roast and then sprinkle the spice mixture on top. Add 1 cup of water to the bottom of the pan before roasting.

3. Place the pork in the oven and cook for 15 minutes. After 15 minutes reduce the oven temperature to 325°F and continue to roast for 1½ to 2 hours, or until a meat thermometer inserted in the middle of the roast registers 145°F degrees for medium or 160°F for well done. Remove the roast from the oven and transfer it to a cutting board. Let the roast rest for 20 minutes before slicing.

As Needed or To Taste: Salt, pepper, paprika, garlic powder, onion powder

Ratatouille

 +  +  +

1 EGGPLANT, CHOPPED   2 ZUCCHINI, SLICED INTO HALF-MOONS   2 BELL PEPPERS, STEMMED, SEEDS AND RIBS REMOVED, AND CHOPPED   4 TOMATOES, SEEDED AND CHOPPED

Directions

1. Coat the bottom of a large cast-iron skillet with olive oil and warm it over medium-high heat. When the oil starts to shimmer, add the eggplant and sauté until pieces are coated with oil and just starting to sizzle, about 2 minutes.

2. Reduce the heat to medium and stir in the zucchini and peppers. Add garlic and a dash of olive oil, cover the skillet, and cook, stirring occasionally, until the eggplant, zucchini, and peppers are almost tender, about 15 minutes.

3. Add the tomatoes, stir to combine, and cook until the eggplant, zucchini, and peppers are tender and the tomatoes have collapsed, about 25 minutes.

4. Remove the skillet from heat, season with salt and pepper, and allow to sit for at least 1 hour. Taste, adjust the seasoning as needed, and reheat the ratatouille before serving.

As Needed or To Taste: Olive oil, minced garlic, salt, pepper

Brown Butter Scallops

24 SCALLOPS

1 STICK OF
UNSALTED BUTTER

3 BUTTERNUT SQUASH,
PEELED, SEEDED, AND DICED

1 CUP RAW,
SHELLED WALNUTS

Directions

1. Place a cast-iron skillet over medium-high heat. Remove the foot from each scallop and discard them. Pat the scallops dry with a paper towel and lightly season both sides with salt and pepper.

2. Add 1 tablespoon of butter to the pan. When it has melted, add the squash, season it with salt and pepper, and cook for 12 to 15 minutes, or until they are tender and caramelized. Remove the squash and set aside.

3. Add the walnuts to the pan and cook, stirring frequently, until the nuts are fragrant, about 2 minutes. Add half of the remaining butter to the pan and cook for 2 to 3 minutes, until it has browned. Pour the walnuts and browned butter into a bowl and set the mixture aside.

4. Place 1 tablespoon of the remaining butter in the pan. Add the scallops one at a time, softly pressing down as you place them in the skillet. Cook the scallops for approximately 3 minutes and then flip them over. The scallops should not stick to the pan when you go to flip them. If the scallops do stick, cook until a brown crust is visible. Once you have flipped the scallops, cook for 2 minutes, remove, and set aside. Add the remaining butter to the pan as needed.

5. Place the squash in the middle of a plate and then place the scallops around and on top of the squash. Spoon the walnuts and browned butter over the dish and garnish with scallions.

As Needed or To Taste: Salt, pepper, chopped scallions

Spaghetti with Zucchini & Pesto

 +  +

1 LB. SPAGHETTI
OR FETTUCCINE

3 ZUCCHINI, TRIMMED
AND SLICED VERY THIN
WITH A MANDOLINE

BASIL PESTO
(SEE PAGE 73)

Directions

1. Bring a large saucepan of water to a boil. When it is boiling, add salt and the pasta and cook until it is nearly al dente, about 7 minutes. When the pasta has 2 minutes left to cook, add the zucchini and stir to combine.

2. Reserve ¼ cup of the cooking water and then drain the pasta and zucchini. Return them to the pot, add the reserved pasta water, and cook over high heat until all of the water has been absorbed. Divide the pasta and zucchini between the plates and top each portion with the pesto.

As Needed or To Taste: Salt

Tofu Tacos

 +  +

1 LB. EXTRA-FIRM TOFU, DRAINED AND CRUMBLED

1 BELL PEPPER, STEMMED, SEEDS AND RIBS REMOVED, AND SLICED

1 TOMATO, CHOPPED

Directions

1. Coat the bottom of a large skillet with olive oil and warm it over medium-high heat. When the oil starts to shimmer, add the tofu, season it with salt, cumin, and garlic powder, and stir until the tofu is thoroughly coated with the spices. Cook until the tofu starts to brown, about 5 minutes. Scramble the tofu in the pan, add the bell pepper, and cook until it starts to soften, about 5 minutes.

2. Add the tomato, drizzle adobo sauce over the mixture, stir to incorporate, and cook for another 5 minutes. Serve with corn tortillas and your preferred taco toppings.

   As Needed or To Taste: Olive oil, salt, cumin, garlic powder, cayenne pepper, adobo sauce, corn tortillas

Desserts

As anyone who has spent a weekend afternoon attempting to make madeleines, macarons, and canelés knows, the process of making something sweet is typically a trying one, requiring scales, careful technique, and extreme patience.

These preparations are far more accessible, allowing you to soothe your cravings quickly when one arises, and build the confidence needed to tackle the classic confections that currently seem so far out of reach.

Bananas Foster

 + +  +

2 STICKS OF UNSALTED BUTTER   **1 CUP FIRMLY PACKED LIGHT BROWN SUGAR**   **6 BANANAS, CUT LENGTHWISE AND HALVED**   **½ CUP DARK RUM**

Directions

1. Place a cast-iron skillet over medium-high heat and add the butter and brown sugar. Once the butter and sugar are melted, add the bananas to the pan and cook until they start to caramelize, about 3 minutes. Spoon the sauce over the bananas as they cook.

2. Remove the pan from heat and add the rum. Using a long match or a wand lighter, carefully ignite the rum. Place the pan back over medium-high heat and shake the pan until the flames have gone out. Stir in cream until the sauce has the desired texture and thickness.

3. Divide the bananas and sauce between the serving dishes. Top each portion with ice cream and cinnamon.

As Needed or To Taste: Heavy cream, vanilla ice cream, cinnamon

Chocolate Mousse

 + **+** **+**

1 CUP BITTERSWEET CHOCOLATE CHIPS   2 CUPS HEAVY CREAM, CHILLED   2 TABLESPOONS SUGAR   3 EGG WHITES

Directions

1. Place the chocolate chips in a microwave-safe bowl and microwave on medium until melted, removing to stir every 15 seconds.

2. Place the cream in a mixing bowl and beat until soft peaks form. Place the sugar and egg whites in another bowl, add vanilla and salt to taste, and beat until soft peaks form.

3. Gradually incorporate the melted chocolate into the egg white mixture. Gently fold in the cream.

4. Transfer the mousse into the serving dishes and refrigerate for at least 1 hour. To serve, top each portion with whipped cream.

    As Needed or To Taste: Vanilla extract, salt, whipped cream

Chocolate-Covered Strawberries

2 PINTS OF FRESH
STRAWBERRIES

2 CUPS SEMISWEET
CHOCOLATE CHIPS

Directions

1. Rinse the strawberries well and pat them dry.

2. Place the chocolate chips in a microwave-safe bowl and microwave on medium until melted, removing to stir every 15 seconds.

3. Dip each strawberry into the chocolate halfway, or completely, whichever you prefer. Roll the coated strawberries in graham cracker crumbs or ground almonds. Line a baking sheet with parchment paper and place the strawberries on the sheet. Place in the refrigerator and chill for at least 2 hours before serving.

As Needed or To Taste: Graham cracker crumbs, finely ground almonds

Chocolate & Walnut Fudge

 +  + +

| 1 LB. QUALITY BITTERSWEET CHOCOLATE, CHOPPED | 1 STICK OF UNSALTED BUTTER | 2 CUPS SUGAR | 1 TEASPOON PURE VANILLA EXTRACT |

Directions

1. Preheat the oven to 350°F and line a square 8-inch cake pan with heavy-duty aluminum foil so that the foil extends over the sides. Spray the foil with nonstick cooking spray.

2. Cover a baking sheet with the desired amount of walnuts, place it in the oven, and toast the walnuts until they are fragrant and lightly browned, about 5 to 7 minutes. Remove from the oven and set the walnuts aside.

3. Place the chocolate and the butter in a heatproof mixing bowl and set aside. Place the sugar in a deep saucepan and cook over medium heat until it has dissolved and is boiling. Continue to cook, while stirring constantly, until the sugar reaches 236°F on a candy thermometer. Carefully pour the sugar over the chocolate-and-butter mixture in the mixing bowl. Whisk until the mixture is smooth and then stir in the toasted walnuts and the vanilla.

4. Spread the fudge in an even layer in the cake pan. Refrigerate the fudge until it is set, about 2 hours. Use the foil to lift the fudge out of the pan and cut the fudge into squares.

As Needed or To Taste: Chopped walnuts

Crème Brûlée

4 CUPS HEAVY CREAM + SEEDS AND POD OF 1 VANILLA BEAN + 1 CUP SUGAR + 6 LARGE EGG YOLKS

Directions

1. Preheat the oven to 325°F. Place the cream, vanilla seeds, and the vanilla pod in a saucepan and bring the mixture to a boil over medium-high heat. Remove the pan from heat, cover it, and let it sit for 15 minutes.

2. Remove the vanilla pod from the mixture and discard it. Place ½ cup of the sugar and the egg yolks in a bowl and whisk until combined. While whisking constantly, add the cream mixture in ¼-cup increments. When all of the cream mixture has been incorporated, divide the mixture between six 8 oz. ramekins.

3. Transfer the ramekins to a 9 x 13–inch baking dish. Pour hot water into the dish until it comes halfway up the sides of the ramekins, place the dish in the oven, and bake until the custard is just set, about 40 minutes. Remove from the oven, transfer the ramekins to the refrigerator, and chill for 2 hours.

4. Remove the ramekins from the refrigerator 30 minutes before you are ready to serve them and allow them to come to room temperature.

5. Divide the remaining sugar between the ramekins and spread evenly on top. Use a kitchen torch to caramelize the sugar, let the crème brulees sit for 5 minutes, and then serve.

As Needed or To Taste: Hot water (120°F)

Affogato

| 1 PINT OF VANILLA ICE CREAM | ¼ CUP KAHLÙA OR SAMBUCA | 1 TEASPOON FRESHLY GRATED NUTMEG | 1¼ CUPS FRESHLY BREWED ESPRESSO OR VERY STRONG COFFEE |

Directions

1. Scoop ice cream into five small glasses. Pour some of the preferred liqueur over each scoop and sprinkle a bit of nutmeg on top.

2. Pour the espresso or coffee over the ice cream. Top each portion with whipped cream and chocolate shavings.

    As Needed or To Taste: Whipped cream, chocolate shavings

Shortbread

 + +  +

| 2½ STICKS OF UNSALTED BUTTER | 10 TABLESPOONS SUGAR | 2½ CUPS ALL-PURPOSE FLOUR | 1 TEASPOON SALT |

Directions

1. Grate the butter into a mixing bowl and place it in the freezer for 30 minutes.

2. Preheat the oven to 325°F. Place ½ cup of the sugar, the flour, salt, and the frozen butter in the work bowl of a stand mixer fitted with the paddle attachment and beat on low until the mixture is fine like sand. Transfer the mixture to a greased square 8-inch cake pan, place it in the oven, and bake until set and golden brown, about 1 hour and 15 minutes.

3. Remove from the oven, sprinkle the remaining sugar over the top, and let the shortbread cool before slicing it into rounds.

Baked Stuffed Apples

 +  + +

6 PINK LADY APPLES · 3 TABLESPOONS UNSALTED BUTTER, MELTED · 6 TABLESPOONS BLACKBERRY JAM · 4 OZ. GOAT CHEESE, CUT INTO 6 ROUNDS

Directions

1. Preheat the oven to 350°F. Slice the tops off of the apples and set them aside. Use a paring knife to cut around the apples' cores and then scoop out the centers. Make sure to leave a ½-inch-thick wall inside the apple.

2. Rub the inside and outside of the apples with some of the melted butter. Place the jam and goat cheese in a mixing bowl and stir to combine. Fill the apples' cavities with the mixture, place the tops back on the apples, and set them aside.

3. Warm a large cast-iron skillet over medium-high heat. Add the remaining butter to the skillet, place the apples in the pan, and place it in the oven. Bake until the apples are tender, 25 to 30 minutes. Remove from the oven and let cool briefly before serving.

Lemon Posset

 + **+** **+**

| 2 CUPS HEAVY CREAM | ⅔ CUP SUGAR | 1 TABLESPOON LEMON ZEST | 6 TABLESPOONS FRESH LEMON JUICE |

Directions

1. Place the heavy cream, sugar, and lemon zest in a saucepan and bring the mixture to a boil over medium heat, stirring constantly. Cook until the sugar has dissolved and the mixture has reduced slightly, about 10 minutes.

2. Remove the saucepan from heat and stir in the lemon juice. Let the mixture stand until a skin forms on the top, about 20 minutes. Strain the mixture through a fine sieve and transfer it to the refrigerator. Chill until set, about 3 hours.

3. About 10 minutes before you are ready to serve the posset, remove the mixture from the refrigerator and let it come to room temperature. Cover the bottom of a serving dish with whipped cream and then alternate layers of the posset and whipped cream. Top each serving with a generous amount of blueberries and serve.

    As Needed or To Taste: Whipped cream, blueberries

Rustico with Honey Glaze

| 4 SHEETS OF FROZEN PUFF PASTRY, THAWED | 1 EGG WHITE, BEATEN | ½ LB. FRESH MOZZARELLA CHEESE, SLICED | 1 CUP HONEY |

Directions

1. Add vegetable oil to a Dutch oven until it is 2 inches deep and warm it to 350°F. Cut eight 5-inch circles and eight 4-inch circles from the sheets of puff pastry. Place a slice of cheese in the center of each 5-inch circle. Place a 4-inch circle over the cheese, fold the bottom circle over the edge, and pinch to seal.

2. Place one or two rustico in the oil and fry until the dough is a light golden brown and crispy, about 2 to 3 minutes. Remove from oil and transfer to a paper towel–lined wire rack. Repeat until all eight wraps have been fried. To serve, drizzle the honey over the top of each rustico.

As Needed or To Taste: Vegetable oil

Peppermint Bark

 +  +  +

| ¾ CUP CRUSHED PEPPERMINT CANDIES | ¾ LB. SEMISWEET CHOCOLATE CHIPS | 2 TEASPOONS VEGETABLE OIL | ¾ LB. WHITE CHOCOLATE CHIPS |

Directions

1. Line a rimmed baking sheet with parchment paper and place the crushed peppermint candies in a mixing bowl.

2. Place the semisweet chocolate chips in a microwave-safe bowl. Microwave on medium until melted, removing to stir every 15 seconds.

3. Stir 1 teaspoon of the vegetable oil into the melted chocolate and then pour the chocolate onto the baking sheet, using a rubber spatula to distribute evenly. Place in the refrigerator until set, about 15 minutes.

4. Place the white chocolate chips in a microwave-safe bowl. Microwave on medium until melted, removing to stir every 15 seconds. Add the remaining oil to the melted white chocolate, stir to combine, and pour the white chocolate mixture on top of the hardened semisweet chocolate, using a rubber spatula to distribute evenly.

5. Sprinkle the peppermint pieces over the white chocolate and lightly press down on them to make sure they adhere. Refrigerate until set, about 30 minutes. Break the bark into pieces and refrigerate until ready to serve.

Bourbon Balls

 +  +  +

2 STICKS OF UNSALTED BUTTER, AT ROOM TEMPERATURE   2 LBS. CONFECTIONERS' SUGAR   ½ CUP BOURBON   ½ TEASPOON SALT

Directions

1. Combine the butter and half of the confectioners' sugar in a mixing bowl and beat at low speed with a handheld mixer to combine. Increase the speed to high and beat until light and fluffy. Add the remaining sugar, bourbon, and salt and beat for 2 minutes. Transfer the mixture to the refrigerator and chill until firm, about 2 hours.

2. Line baking sheets with parchment paper and form tablespoons of the butter-and-bourbon mixture into balls. Coat the balls in melted chocolate, cocoa powder, and/or shredded coconut and then transfer the sheets to the refrigerator. Chill for 45 minutes before serving.

As Needed or To Taste: Melted chocolate, cocoa powder, shredded coconut

Mille-Feuille

+

+

+

2 SHEETS OF FROZEN
PUFF PASTRY, THAWED

PASTRY CREAM
(SEE SIDEBAR)

ZEST OF 1 ORANGE

1 TABLESPOON
GRAND MARNIER

Directions

1. Preheat the oven to 400°F. Roll out the sheets of puff pastry and place each one on a greased baking sheet. Dust the sheets with confectioners' sugar, place them in the oven, and bake for 12 to 15 minutes, until golden brown. Remove from the oven, transfer to a wire rack, and let cool.

2. Place the Pastry Cream in a bowl, add the orange zest and Grand Marnier, and fold to incorporate. Transfer the mixture into a piping bag and place it in the refrigerator to chill while the puff pastry continues to cool.

3. Divide each sheet of the cooled puff pastry into 3 equal portions. Remove the piping bag from the freezer and place a thick layer of cream on one of the pieces of puff pastry. Dot the edges of the cream with raspberries and press down on them gently. Fill the space between the raspberries with more of the cream and place another piece of puff pastry on top. Repeat the process with the cream and raspberries and then place the last piece of puff pastry on top. Carefully cut into the desired number of portions and serve.

As Needed or To Taste: Confectioners' sugar, raspberries

Pastry Cream

Place 2 cups whole milk and 1 tablespoon unsalted butter in a saucepan and bring to a simmer over medium heat. As the mixture is coming to a simmer, place ½ cup granulated sugar and 3 tablespoons cornstarch in a small bowl and whisk to combine. Add 2 large eggs and whisk until the mixture is smooth and creamy. While stirring constantly, gradually incorporate half of the milk mixture into the egg mixture. Add a pinch of kosher salt and ½ teaspoon pure vanilla extract, stir to incorporate, and pour the tempered eggs into the saucepan. Cook, stirring constantly, until the mixture is thick enough to coat the back of a wooden spoon. Make sure not to let the mixture come to a boil. Pour the cream into a bowl, place plastic wrap directly on the surface to prevent a skin from forming, and refrigerate until cool.

Honey Nut Truffles

 **+** **+** **+**

½ CUP PEANUT BUTTER   ¼ CUP HONEY   ¼ TEASPOON SALT   1 CUP QUALITY SEMISWEET CHOCOLATE CHIPS

Directions

1. Place the peanut butter, honey, and salt in a bowl and stir until well combined. Form teaspoons of the mixture into balls and place them on a parchment-lined baking sheet. Place them in the refrigerator and chill for 1 hour.

2. Remove the baking sheet from the refrigerator. Place the chocolate chips in a microwave-safe bowl and microwave on medium until melted, removing to stir every 15 seconds.

3. Dip the balls in the melted chocolate until completely covered. Place them back on the baking sheet. When all of the truffles have been coated, refrigerate until the chocolate is set.

Muddy Buddies

+

+

+

| 1 CUP SEMISWEET CHOCOLATE CHIPS | ¾ CUP CREAMY PEANUT BUTTER | 9 CUPS RICE CHEX | 1½ CUPS CONFECTIONERS' SUGAR |

Directions

1. Place the chocolate chips and peanut butter in a microwave-safe bowl and microwave on medium until the mixture is melted, removing to stir every 15 seconds. Remove from the microwave, add the desired amount of vanilla, and stir until the mixture is smooth.

2. Place the Chex in a large mixing bowl and pour the peanut butter-and-chocolate mixture over the cereal. Gently stir until all of the cereal has been coated.

3. Place the mixture in a large resealable plastic bag and add the confectioners' sugar. Seal the bag and shake until each piece of Chex is coated with sugar. Pour the mixture onto a parchment-lined baking sheet and refrigerate for 45 minutes before serving.

As Needed or To Taste: Pure vanilla extract

Metric Conversions

U.S. Measurement	Approximate Metric Liquid Measurement	Approximate Metric Dry Measurement
1 teaspoon	5 ml	5 g
1 tablespoon or ½ ounce	15 ml	14 g
1 ounce or ⅛ cup	30 ml	29 g
¼ cup or 2 ounces	60 ml	57 g
⅓ cup	80 ml	76 g
½ cup or 4 ounces	120 ml	113 g
⅔ cup	160 ml	151 g
¾ cup or 6 ounces	180 ml	170 g
1 cup or 8 ounces or ½ pint	240 ml	227 g
1½ cups or 12 ounces	350 ml	340 g
2 cups or 1 pint or 16 oz.	475 ml	454 g
3 cups or 1½ pints	700 ml	680 g
4 cups or 2 pints or 1 quart	950 ml	908 g

Index

About Cider Mill Press Book Publishers

Good ideas ripen with time. From seed to harvest, Cider Mill Press brings fine reading, information, and entertainment together between the covers of its creatively crafted books. Our Cider Mill bears fruit twice a year, publishing a new crop of titles each spring and fall.

"Where Good Books Are Ready for Press"

Visit us on the web at

cidermillpress.com

or write to us at

PO Box 454
12 Spring St.
Kennebunkport, Maine 04046